THE ABUNDANT MAMA'S GUIDE TO SAVORING SLOW

Embrace
the
Chaos!

♡
Shawn

"Not a day goes by that I don't still need to remind myself that my life is not just what's handed to me, nor is it my list of obligations, my accomplishments or failures, or what my family is up to, but rather it is what I choose, day in and day out, to make of it all. When I am able simply to be with things as they are, able to accept the day's challenges without judging, reaching, or wishing for something else, I feel as if I am receiving the privilege, coming a step closer to being myself. It's when I get lost in the day's details, or so caught up in worries about what might be, that I miss the beauty of what is." ~ Katrina Kenison, *The Gift of an Ordinary Day: A Mother's Memoir*

"Write it on your heart that every day is the best day in the year."
~ Ralph Waldo Emerson

For Dan, Jadyn and Liana — three of the best reasons I've ever found to ban busy and begin savoring slow.

Contents

Introduction to Savoring Slow

"I am beginning to learn that it is the sweet, simple things of life which are the real ones after all." ~ Laura Ingalls Wilder

***

Imagine waking up, drinking your coffee and listening to the birds on your front porch.

You take a quick walk around and note the grass is tall enough for mowing, how the dandelions have turned to seed and that there are several types of birds in your front yard.

This is not the life of a retiree.

This is my life.

With two children and a husband who commutes two hours a day and sometimes works 12-hour days.

The children are busy in children busyness ways. Making messes. Asking questions. Suggesting we do this or that.

And yet we have found a way to stop in the mornings to savor the life we have before us right now.

Because we know it will not last forever, that at any moment this could end.

Busyness is a state of mind.

In fact, we're all so busy it's not enough to just tell our friends and write it on social media. We are now busy diagnosing our overwhelmed, maxed-out and busy-trapped lives. We almost feel obligated to tell people we're busy, even if we're not that busy at all.

In the last several years as a mother, I have tried on all the possible ways of motherhood.

I've been a stay-at-home mom. I've been a working mom. And I've been a work-at-home mama.

Guess what?

I have always been busy, too busy to do everything I wanted to do. But I've also rarely felt that busy, and that's because I have been savoring the slow parts of this amazing journey of raising a family.

I may not ever completely reach the end of my own list of personal goals and dreams, but I have never wasted a single day doing anything that wasn't important while raising my twin daughters. It's all been important. It may not always feel that way at the time, but it is, and embracing it all is simply Savoring Slow.

When we forget this, we enter into the crazed state of busyness.

Perhaps you suffer from busyness, too. It's that syndrome when you are constantly lacking time and wishing for more of it. It might be why you picked up this book. Maybe you are constantly too tired to do what you want to do. Constantly feeling overwhelmed and not even sure why. Constantly maxed out on life's stresses.

Here are several reasons you might be feeling that way:

- **We think too much.** We over-analyze situations. We read into people's thoughts and behaviors. We focus on our faults —

and others' faults. We spend countless hours on matters we cannot change.

- **We worry too much.** We put too much energy and time into things like what our child is wearing, eating, not eating, saying, not saying. We put too much time into who is doing what, who hasn't done what and what needs to be done next.

- **We're too focused on others.** What is he thinking? Why is she crying? When will she finally walk/talk/be potty trained? Why is he miserable? When will he help me more?

- **We plan too much.** We're very, very busy striving for perfection so we can snap a picture of it and put it on Facebook. The perfect meal. The perfect craft. The perfect living room arrangement and decor. The perfect outfit. Just what are we going to do that is so amazing today?

- **We try to do too much.** If we could just do the laundry, finish that project, walk the dog, play a game with the kids, make dinner, read the library book that's overdue and take an hour to work out this morning we'd be just fine. Really.

All of this mental work our brains are doing all day — thinking about everyone else — is actually eating up our time and it's depleting our energy. All that mental work is also more likely to make you feel things like guilt, shame, doubt, anger and fear — none of which make for a happy, healthy and slow day.

But I know what you are thinking.

You need your busy life. You need it like air. Because when you're not busy, the kids go crazy. They fight. And whine. And cling to you.

All across the world right this minute there are hundreds of children being tugged, pulled and torn in many different directions. They are being force-fed educational learning activities, games and challenges. They are being dragged to stores to buy many things and rushed off to sports to enrich their lives for the better.

And many more tugging and pulling their parents in a million different directions because they don't know how to just be without doing, without planning the next thing.

These children are stressed, over-scheduled and tired.

And so are their parents.

Many of us realize that the busyness culture of families today doesn't feel right, and we'd like to put the brakes on rather quickly in the fast lane of life.

But how?

Why Savoring Slow?

It was one of those carefully written emails. I slowly and cautiously typed an email to some mom friends of my daughters' previous school. We had moved mid-year after realizing the school wasn't the right fit any longer. But we wanted to keep their friendships strong — the ones they had built during their first three years in school.

Perhaps a Saturday morning park date? With coffee and donuts? When the weather is nice. Make it if you can. See you next time if you can't.

"Darn, we can't, the girls have Chinese lessons," one mom wrote back instantly.

"Sorry, swimming class all morning, how about another time?" another chimed in.

"Soccer!" another said.

That's when it occurred to me that we might be the only unscheduled family in America.

Modern family life is a constant whirlwind of dos and don'ts. Our days revolve around what we have to do and what we'd like to do and what we'll, sadly, never get to do today.

Modern family life is a constant juggle of needs and wants. Our days revolve around how much time we should or should not spend on technology in our homes and in our life.

Modern family life is a constant rush of responsibilities that involves growing expenses, growing fears and growing needs.

Our culture of busyness is to blame

Savoring Slow is about changing your mindset about what is important so you can leave more space in your day for those things that matter.

Savoring Slow is about showing up for the good stuff and letting go of the not-so-good stuff. (Tweet this.)

Savoring Slow is about a life of abundance that just really starts to flow your way, and you don't have to feel like you are chasing a dream anymore.But where do you fin the slow parts?

It's found in your faith and spirituality. It's found in your sense of wonder. It's found in your willingness to be patient and creative. It's found in your imagination. It's found at the margins of your day where you slip outside just before bed to stare at the stars because you need that glimpse as if it's the breath to add space between your ribs.

This book is going to walk you through the 12 Habits to Savoring Slow. Perhaps you already know that the secret to slowing down is simply realizing you woke up to a precious 24-hour gift that is only redeemable today and so you are going to savor it slowly.

You are tired of people telling you to slow down. You need permission to slow down. You need ideas on how to slow down. You need to feel empowered to feel less rushed.

But how do you get there? What do you need to do more of to feel that slow, easy feeling you long to feel?

Perhaps you have already begun asking yourself what you want to say at the end of your life about how you lived and you're realizing that you need to get out of the fast lane right now — maybe your health depends on it, or maybe your child's disappointed eyes seeing you at the computer, again, is what is calling you right now.

Perhaps you already know your time is sacred, your time is precious, and your time is a gift.

So let's stop saying we're too busy and start savoring slow instead.

The Abundant Mama's Guide to Savoring Slow is here to guide you in a different direction that when implemented will actually give you the results you are seeking right now in your life.

We're off ramping and leaning out of the busy culture in order to take back our time, but we're doing it with balance and intention.

This book is going to give you ample amounts of permission to let go of the fast lane and the busy life and slow it down while also remaining connected to what matters most in your life.

Slowing down is how we find more hours in the day. Not real hours — not the ones on the clock, per se — but the hours that feel good. The hours that mean so much to us.

There are many ways to slow time even in a busy life.

Because I'm not here to tell you to stop your busy life.

I'm here to inspire you to savor the life you have.

Time slows when we put all of our senses into a moment. When we notice the lighting, the way their clothes hang on their body, the smell of the rain, the sounds of the birds outside. Time slows when we taste our food on all sides of our tongues.

Time slows when we notice the details of the way the moon hangs in the sky or the way the stars drip like diamonds falling out of a universe we'll never fully understand. Or how our child's knees grew knobbier over the winter.

Time slows when we notice how precious every moment really feels.

Time slows when we are doing what we love so much we are willing to put in the time — no matter how long it takes. Putting on a Band-aid, for instance, or making a birthday cake. We love it so much we are willing to put our whole being — our mind, body and spirit — into that moment.

Time slows when we understand and appreciate why we are here in this moment.

Time slows when we stop to savor all of it. The noise. The chaos. The beauty. The simple. The boring.

Perhaps then the secret lies not in getting more hours but in appreciating the hours we already have.

And that's what Savoring Slow is all about.

The 12 Habits of Savoring Slow

In my life, both as a busy journalist and working mom and now as a business owner and writer, I have always been a go-getter. Entirely motivated to take on the world at all times.

And productive. I've always been extremely productive. I can run circles around many people who are trying to do the same work at the same time.

And yet you will find no one more dedicated and motivated to seeking out the awe in life. I could sit and watch the world unfold all day long. I could people-watch all day long.

I've been given a gift of seeing the world through a different kind of lens and that lens only works when I live a Savoring Slow life and use the Savoring Slow Habits outlined in this book. This book is set up for you to work on one habit per month but if you work at a faster pace — while also retaining the information and starting the habit — you can move through it more quickly.

Experts and researchers have repeatedly said it takes up to 30 days of practicing a new habit for it to stick. Same goes for trying to break a bad habit.

As you work your way through each of these habits, make them your priority for the month — not for a day. Over time, you will find the practice of these Savoring Slow habits easier and more achievable.

1. Wake Up — Practice waking up every single day to see the beauty in your life.
2. Release — Embrace the idea of letting go of what is not working for you any longer to create more time for what you love.
3. Reframe — Accept that your busy life is your beautiful life and start telling yourself a different story about how you are living.
4. Focus — Aim for a distraction-free life where you always try to do one thing or nothing at all.
5. Go Slowly — Forget rushing through and start lingering more in all areas of your day.
6. Do Less — Understand that the only way to have more time for the good stuff is to do less of the other stuff.

7. Plug-in — Reject the notion that you need to unplug and start intentionally plugging in to be more efficient with your time and life.

8. Unstructured — Create more free time in your family's day to allow the wow moments to evolve and multiply.

9. Go Quiet — Quiet your mind and feel time expand in the process.

10. Savor — Take time to appreciate every little detail around you.

11. Abundance — Start seeing time for what it is — something to be thankful for in your life.

12. Make Space — Carve out physical, mental and emotional space in your life for the things you want more of in your day.

As with anything, read everything with a grain of salt, release what doesn't work for you and put into motion those things that do. Change and alter the exercises to fit your life and your family. Everything in this book is achievable whether you work or work-from-home.

It's just a simple method of changing your perspective — and a few bad habits.

How to use this book:

The mission of this book is not to tell you to get off the grid and leave busyness behind forever. It's to show you how to live in a way that makes this life meaningful. It's to wake you up to every possibility that you do have so you can remember to seize the good before the bad takes over.

Through the pages of this book, we're really just making time and space in our lives to do what we love to do while also making time and space to love what we have to do.

The first two chapters will help you prepare for this journey. You have to be ready. Your family has to be ready. Without these two vital first steps, you will find ditching the busy trap much harder to do.

After that, each chapter will offer a new habit to begin. The habits are tangible ways where you can literally — and emotionally — begin to slow down.

At the end, you also will have created a blueprint that is unique to your family about what it means to live the Savoring Slow habits.

And you will do it all at your own pace because nothing in your life — not even this book — is worth rushing through.

Replenish Yourself First

_____

"People who keep stiff upper lips find that it's damn hard to smile." — Judith Guest.

***

I have never met more resistance from the mothers I coach than when I suggest they take time to just do nothing and rest for a few minutes each day.

The idea of relaxing and letting go is scary.

The idea of facing ourselves in a moment of solitude is scary.

The idea of releasing our inner serious person is scary.

All of this is why meditation is not only hard to sit down and do but also hard to sit through.

Too many thoughts, ideas and things to do crowd our brain.

Thinking and doing is so natural and normal to us that we don't really know how to be without thinking and doing.

And yet, really, that's what we long for in life, isn't it? More time to just be?

So if that's what we long for, why aren't we making more time for it? Why aren't we choosing to do more of that even when we know we have the time?

Such as: Instead of spending 15 minutes on Facebook, maybe I'll just sit down and relax in the quiet.

Doing nothing through our days truly is the key to feeling less crazy busy. Even just taking a five-minute break each day can really turn around your feelings of overwhelm.

It's a mind game, really.

In fact, the answer to slowing down really is more in our control than we think.

To prepare to slow down, we often gear up, declutter and clean. We nest. And plan. And create. We call people. And buy things.

We make ourselves crazy, in other words.

Think of the last time you planned a nice, relaxing vacation? Not so relaxing to get ready for, right? Not so relaxing to pack and unpack, right?

In Savoring Slow, getting ready to slow down means nothing more than mentally preparing for a slower pace. Your life really isn't going to be that much slower, but your perception of your crazy life will be much different, at least if you are doing it right.

Before you can move forward with a plan of action on a slower life, you must first get your mind, body and soul ready for a different way of life — one that leaves more room for your own self-care and needs.

Why?

Mothers are the backbone of our homes. We must be grounded and centered in what we envision before we can move on to share this with the rest of the family.

The sections of this chapter are going to walk you through what you can do to get ready, personally, for a slower life.

Start a slow-sleeping routine

Most of the time, when we say we're busy, what we mean is that we're busy doing things we don't want to do. We're busy doing all those obligations and adult responsibilities that aren't any fun.

This probably includes that block of self-care time you desperately need.

Slowing down to allow more time for ourselves is one of the hardest parts of being a mother. We want to make sure everyone else is OK, so we often neglect what our mind, body and soul needs most.

Begin with getting more sleep.

To fit more in, we always stay up late because that's the best time to finally get to those things we've been unable to do while caring for the family.

But sleep really is the answer to being more awake for your life and having more energy to fit it all in. A well-rested mother is more likely to feel like she has more time and energy for the good stuff than one who wakes at the last minute and rushes to fit it all in with a bitter and sour attitude.

There are many nights when I have so much to do, and I almost don't know what to pick first, and then I notice that really I am just exhausted.

And so, I choose sleep. Often, on those nights, I am wrapped up in my blankets with my gratitude journal and a good book by 8:30 p.m. When I do this once or twice a week, the week just flows so much better for me.

Savoring Slow Invitation: During the course of this book, keep a sleep log. Begin tracking your own sleep patterns. Write down what time you go to sleep and what time you wake up (and how). How many total hours did you sleep? Make a note of how you feel during the day as well. Over time, you should start to see what times work best for you to sleep. For fun, have your children keep their own sleep logs. There are now apps and small devices to help track your sleep cycles as well such as FitBit and the Sleep Cycle app.

Let rest flow through your day

Sleeping is great, but sometimes, no matter how much you get, you still feel tired and overwhelmed from such a busy day. That's why I always suggest to moms that they build in more rest throughout the day.

A couple years ago, I took a meditation class where the very first meditation was not a traditional meditation.

Instead, we were encouraged to simply sit and wait.

Wait as if you are waiting on a nest of eggs to hatch beneath you.

I have done this meditation many times since and have adapted it to serve my own needs and over time I have given it its own name — my Savoring Slow meditation.

If thoughts arise during this meditation rather than chase them away and stifle them, you follow them for a while. And then watch them go.

The first time I tried this type of meditation — after years of traditional meditation practice where you are trying to not think while sitting uncomfortably on a cushion — I was changed.

To just sit and let my thoughts form fully and completely around me rather than chase them way, rather than act on them, rather than make something happen was so completely liberating.

I sit in this Savoring Slow meditation quite frequently. Because I have a busy mind and, to be honest, it's a good thing for me. I love that I have an active mind with a lot of ideas and thoughts. I make things happen with those ideas.

But what I hadn't been giving myself time for was the ability to just let them flutter along like a bee, pollinating the landscape with beauty. They are always interrupted by something or someone, especially by my own doing.

By letting the thoughts form completely, they seem to hold less power over me and my day.

It might seem silly to meditate as if you are sitting on a nest of eggs, but it feels right to finally just be, to not force anything away and not be required to do anything more than just sit and think.

To just be.

Savoring Slow Invitation: Take 10 minutes today to sit in this Savoring Slow meditation. To practice the Savoring Slow meditation sit quietly in a comfortable seated position. Take a few deep breaths before you get started. And sit peacefully and wait for several breaths.

Savoring Slow Meditation

To practice this Savoring Slow meditation simply find a

comfortable seated position, perhaps in your favorite chair by a window or even outside.

- Take a few deep breaths, the kind you feel in your upper back.

- Let your body relax. Let your face and jaw relax.

- Close your eyes.

- Breathe into the tension in your shoulders and neck a few times. Breathe into the tension in your lower back.

- Do a few neck rolls to release even more tension from your neck.

- Listen to the sounds around you and notice them. Listen for the birds and other signs of life. Notice how the birds aren't busy doing anything but eating and singing their song.

- Just keep breathing. If a thought forms, watch it flutter along without resistance.

- Watch the thought form. Watch it fold and refold in on itself. Watch how it evolves. And if you notice fear or worry or doubt rising with the fear, take a deep breath.

- It's only a thought. Let the thought go as it needs to go. Don't steer it. Don't converse with it. Don't try and change it. Don't make a list in your head to act on it.

- Just follow it.

- And then let it go.

- After a few cycles of this, allow yourself to slowly start to wiggle and return to the physical space around you. Slowly become aware of the sounds around you. Blink your eyes to wake up and notice first where you are and how you are seated and how your hands are rested and relaxed.

- Return to your day slowly. Feel free to now write about anything that popped up for you in that meditation.

Create a slow ritual around ordinary tasks

You just walked into a room and walked out and didn't do what you set out to do.

You just drove to the bank and have no memory of the turns you made.

We do the same things over and over again, and these habits help us do everything done we need to do. These habits get us through our days and from place to place. These tasks are the bulk of our days, actually.

It's no wonder, then, why we get to the end of the day wondering where our time went.

Perhaps it went so quickly because we weren't awake and aware for any of it — or at least for most of it.

One of my favorite ways to turn a routine into something more meaningful is to create a ritual around it that I can turn to every day. This is a great way to create meaningful, intentional habits to replace others that may not feel so healthy.

For instance, I have created a morning ritual for myself that feels just right, that provides me with the early morning nourishment and relaxation I need. For a long time, I would struggle with what to do if I rose early, ahead of the kids. Walk? That's great, but it's usually dark and walking in the dark isn't appealing to me. Plan my day? Helpful, but not nourishing. Finally, I settled on a sky watch while drinking coffee followed by morning journaling.

This is a powerful ritual to start my day, every day — weekends included.

Creating a ritual can be so simple and enjoyable, it opens up a whole new world to a really boring task.

> Savoring Slow Invitation: Pick one ordinary routine or task you have to do each day (shower, wash dishes, fold laundry, change a diaper, feed a baby, sweep the floor) and create a ritual around that moment. Light a candle and turn on some tunes. Put some really special lotion on after you wash the dishes. Listen to a meditation podcast while folding laundry.

Meditate without meditating

Until this year, I wanted to be that woman meditating.

I wanted to feel that peace. I wanted to be that mindful and purposeful in my everyday moments.

But getting myself to the pillow was so hard, and the more I didn't do it, the more guilt I felt.

So after a while I gave up on it.

And even now that I can easily meditate for up to 40 minutes at a time, I am reminded of those days when I just released this as my goal.

Instead, I took up daily meditation in other places and spaces because that was more possible with my busy mom schedule.

You don't have to sit on a cushion for hours to stay awake and be mindful.

You can simply focus on every moment of your day as if it is your last one. Your day as a mother, in fact, has many moments that are ripe for meditation and attention.

Zen is the art of noticing, observing, paying attention to the moment you are in right now — not thinking about the past or the future, which is where so many of us spend our mental energy.

This section is going to inspire you to find the least likely spaces in your day when you can reduce the noise and the thoughts in your mind and just be. When you find yourself doing any of these everyday tasks, make a point to give yourself permission to slip into a meditative state of not thinking, not doing, not dreaming, not planning and just being one with your body and mind.

Taking a shower: Normally, a busy mom doesn't think of a shower as a place of meditation. Refuge, maybe, but not necessarily meditation. However, in this one moment of our days, we are given the one thing we need most: privacy. At least for some of that time. Physically imagining the water washing over your mind and rinsing away your worries is a powerful way to start — or end — a busy day. Letting fears wash away can open new spaces in your mind so that when you are done and dry and ready to go about your ordinary routine you will feel more grounded and centered. The key, though, as to all of these unique spaces, is to be in the moment fully for as long as you can be there.

Doing the laundry: The second you pull a warm towel out of the dryer and bring it in close and smell it, that moment is a potential for meditation. To let every worry and fear go and just relax into the bliss of folding towels. When I fold laundry with all of my senses, I am in that moment and nothing else really seems to matter.

Washing the dishes: Just like doing the laundry, washing the dishes is a perfect time to awaken all of your senses, a perfect time to stare out the window or at a beautiful painting you've hung near the sink. We need to make more time for sinking into a moment like this where our hands are busy doing and our minds are allowed to rest and be idle for a while.

Watering the flowers: Anyone can have plants, though, I haven't had indoor plants in a long time. The art of watering flowers or plants, indoors or out, is a mindful one as well. You have to pay attention to how much or how little, and you will also notice the other details of what is for these living beings. And while you do all of that, your mind has instantly detached from your other to-dos for a while.

Putting a child to sleep: Many little children want their parents to stick around for a while after lights out. They are afraid or worried or just reluctant to be alone from us. This is a great time to get settled into a comfortable position and sit with your quiet thoughts and breathe. You are doing a good thing for your child by being there, and you are doing a good thing for yourself by just being.

Walking to the mailbox or around the block: Walking anywhere is a great time to put away the worries and to-dos and just live in the moment. As you are walking, notice what you are doing and what you see and say it all in your mind — or even out loud. Noticing and paying attention to what you see all around you allows your mind to rest. This kind of walking can be done while walking to get the mail or walking a dog or walking around the block or along the beach or in the woods. The location matters not at all, but the quality of your mind on that walk matters a ton.

Getting Your Family on Board

"We all have the same 24/7. What we do with our time becomes our priority. Choose what you do with your time and do not lead a life by default" — Patt Hollinger Pickett

***

I'll never forget the day my husband Dan — after years of watching me write in my own gratitude journal — started his own nightly gratitude journal.

It was like a switch finally came on, and he saw the value of something I'd been doing for a long, long time.

But this was only after years of me suggesting he start one and years of him putting it off. Not to be disrespectful, but he just wasn't sure it was for him and, of course, he was too busy.

One of the most common questions I get asked from the mothers I work with is, "How do I get my whole family to agree on this?"

This includes children, too. And it encompasses everything from slowing down to practicing gratitude to setting a family budget.

In an ideal world, everyone would always agree on what is best for a family.

Families would never argue. Homes would always be well taken care of because everyone agrees on what needs to be done at the same time every day.

But this isn't our reality.

Can you imagine how boring that would be anyway?

So before we can even begin this Savoring Slow journey to ban busy and start Savoring Slow, we must figure out how to make this a whole-family experience.

And it's also really important to stress that, like everything in life, this process will not be perfect. It will take much trial and error. And patience. And cheerleading. And motivation.

The end result, though, will be a more peaceful family. Not peaceful days, necessarily, but a more peaceful family overall.

So how do you try to get your family on board?

This chapter will walk you through some steps that will get you closer to that end goal.

Understand when your family needs a recharge

The authors of the book "Simplicity Parenting" caught my attention years ago when they discussed soul fevers in kids and how we can see the symptoms in children who are suffering and in need of love and care — as if they had the flu.

Like a physical fever, soul fevers also have symptoms. Children can behave in ways that show they are out of sorts emotionally, when they anger easily or have trouble sleeping.

Well, if a child can suffer a soul fever, so can a family. A family's bout of this case of the doldrums — or blahs — often feels like something we all refer to as a funk. Something you just can't shake but you really, really hope it passes soon. This is just one of the many seasons we all go through.

Like a soul fever in a child, there are plenty of symptoms of a family that needs a recharge.

- Yelling and snapping at each other.

- Rushing here and there.

- Waking up late or not sleeping well at night.

- Poor eating habits.

- Getting sick a lot.

- Having trouble at work or in school.

- Increased sibling rivalry.

- Forgetting things and missing appointments.

- Pent up anger and resentment.

Savoring Slow Invitation: Pay attention to when your children are acting up or when you are feeling zapped of energy. Write down all the symptoms your family has right now. Come up with a special, slow way to be still and try and re-energize yourselves.

Once you know your family's rhythms and quirks, you can start to easily recognize a family funk and how to deal with it appropriately.

Sometimes, what you need is rest. Or a good family meal full of your favorite comfort foods. A good laugh. A long day trip out of town. Or, perhaps, just a really long chat.

At our house, a funk is almost always eased by going upstairs right after dinner and gathering around one bed and laughing and resting and just being together. This doesn't happen in five minutes. It takes a good hour or two to really see the benefits and the shifts it makes in our family unit.

Creating modern family values in this really busy, fast-paced world is not easy. We're pulled in many directions with technology, resources, entertainment and ideas and we're more influenced by others now more than ever thanks to social media.

And we're left asking ourselves a lot of questions. Doubting ourselves completely. Wondering if we're failing our children. It's easy to get confused. It's easy to feel conflicted. Torn. Which way is best? What path should we take? What is our next move? But all those questions are exhausting. All of those internal debates are exhausting and burning us out even more.

Stop second-guessing and ask yourself in any moment what is most important?

Here are some examples of when to bring out this question: What is more important?

- Cleaning the floors or taking a walk?

- Being on the computer or reading?

- Being right or being kind?

- Being perfect or being real?

- Being loved or being accepted?

- Being helped or being told?

- Being empowered or being changed?

- Being available or being busy?

- The phone or the person on the phone?

- The status update or living the life behind the status update?

- Answering that email or answering that plea for another book?

- Cleaning up the house or binge watching that new series everyone's talking about?

- Looking good or feeling good?

- Saying yes or saying no?

- Trusting yourself or trusting others?

- Doing what is best for you or doing what is best for others?

- Waiting or taking charge of a situation?

- Being in charge or being understanding?

- Talking or listening?

- Taking a deep breath or running out of breath?

- Being here now or being everywhere?

Savoring Slow Invitation — Assess your life as a family. What one moment stands out to you as the most magical and amazing? Pick that one moment and write a love letter to that moment. Tell that moment why you loved it so much, how you felt and why you appreciated it so much. And be sure to add why you need more moments like that in your life.

Establishing a Slow Table Talks

One other surefire way my family snaps out of a funk — when we feel swallowed up by disorganized chaos or poor communication or negative attitudes — is calling a meeting. Now our daughters love our family meetings. But that's because we've made them super fun and light.

You can do that, too.

First, to make your family meeting fun, you can't call it a meeting. In fact, we're going to do a lot of mind trickery in this section. This is the first trick. Never, ever give a boring name to something you have to do.

What I love about a Slow Table Talks is the energy this kind of fun meeting can bring to a family that has been feeling disconnected or dealing with a lot of chaos.

There are rules for these Slow Table Talks, though.

1. Assign job duties with fancy titles. (Think Behavior Management Specialist, Yummy Snack Producer, Joy Campaign Manager)
2. Offer yummy food (put the kids in charge of this).

3. Make it fun.
4. Make it meaningful.

Let's be real. This is great for younger children, but if you have tweens or teens who don't play these games, just have a meeting on the couch with a lot of snacks and drinks with the promise of a movie later. Or take a ride and have this conversation in the car while heading out on a day trip. The point is not where it happens. The point is that the conversations just happen whenever and wherever.

The very last thing you want to feel is stress or pressure at a meeting to try and get your family on board for a slower, more meaningful life.

Here are a few examples of Slow Table Talk topics to cover in your first few chats.

Your First Slow Table Talk | Create a Family Values List

As we drove in our car on a 10-hour trip for a vacation, I wrote down every single thing that was important to us as a family. The list had about 10 items on it — enough to be meaningful, but not overwhelming.

A week later, I took those notes and turned them into a tiny book that we kept on our bedroom dresser for years, a touchstone to the family we wanted to be. That list of values has not changed one bit and it's been several years.

Not sure what your values are? Ask these questions to your family members.

• What do you want to feel like each day in our family and at home? [energized. peaceful. loved. connected. motivated. balanced.]

- How do others see our family? [peaceful. happy. giving. centered. grounded. full of light.]

- What words do you think we can use to describe our family? [strong. peaceful. creative. energetic. motivated. successful. loving. caring. compassionate.]

- What does an ideal day feel like to us? [playful. meaningful. connected. relaxed. busy. full. lively. simple. slow.]

- What do we need more of at home? [laugh. play. exercise. meditate. connect. reach out to someone. ask for help. recharge.]

Let this meeting rest here. Eat the snacks and let everything else go for now. This exercise can easily be done in the car. At the drive-in waiting for the movie to start. In a restaurant waiting for dinner to arrive. In the backyard sitting on a blanket watching the stars.

Your Second Slow Table Talk | Set a Slow Intention

It's so easy to let busyness creep back in, so this book — and these slow family habits — are a practice. You can once-and-done all of the work in this book, but if you don't set an intention and stick to it, you will find yourselves back in a new meeting six months from now wondering where the time went.

A slow family intention declares how you want to feel as a family as you slow down and put more meaningful moments in your days.

Here are some sample intentions you can use for brainstorming your own ideas.

- Our family wants to feel active and healthy this year. May this year be filled with more fresh air and joyful energy.

- May our family spend our days feeling peaceful and slow this year. May we celebrate and honor activities and events that bring us together, not apart.

- Our family feels happiest when we spend time together. May we make more time for things that bring us all joy.

Your Third Slow Table Talk | Choose a Slow Family Word of the Year

One of the more fun things we've done as a family is create a word of the year. Our word was wonder. And it still sits front and center in our lives. And when the word pops up, it's always a fun spark to our imaginations.

Finding a word to all agree on might be easier than you think. Start by having everyone choose two or three words they would love to be the word of the year. And then vote on those words to bring your list down to two or three. And then vote again to see which will be the winner.

Your Fourth Slow Table Talk | Set Slow Family Goals

If the signs of the family funk have been appearing and re-appearing, it's time to set some goals to slow down and take better care of yourselves.

It's easy to feel motivated in a group. And what better support system than loving family members who know all of your flaws and imperfections?

At this week's Talk, simply ask for each member to set a goal that matters to them — something that will benefit that person and the whole family. Common goals: Eat more meals together, walk more, get home earlier, spend less time on a device or watching TV or be kinder to each other.

Savoring Slow Invitation — Take time to carefully plan out a list of Slow Table Talk ideas you want to bring up to your family. Going into each Talk with a list of conversation starters can be helpful to keep everyone engaged. Brainstorm your ideas on paper and cross out what you want to save for another Slow Table Talk.

Savoring Slow Habit No. 1 | Wake Up

The moments I hold most dear are those that arise unbidden in the course of any day — small, evanescent, scarcely worth noticing except for the fact that I am being offered, just for a second, a glimpse into another's soul." ~ Katrina Kenison, in "Mitten Strings for God: Reflections For Mothers In A Hurry."

***

I always know when it's time to slow down.

I feel it like a storm coming on through the sky. The energy in my whole body changes. My muscles start to clench and hurt. I grind my teeth at night while sleeping. I walk around hyped up, anxious and full of nervous vibrations.

And yet, I'm utterly exhausted. I have found, though, that these moments are less and less frequent when I am living in a way that puts all of my love and attention into the current moment and the people with whom I spend time.

I call this being awesomely awake. This is the first step I took on my own intentional journey toward a slower, more meaningful family life. And that's why our first Savoring Slow Habit is to simply wake up.

Waking up doesn't mean literally waking up in the morning, though that is a part of the process. Waking up means opening your eyes, your ears, your feelings, your tastes and your nose to all areas of delight around you. Waking up means bringing all you've got to a moment — to a single task — and relishing it with all your being.

This doesn't mean I do not have plans. I do. Big plans, in fact. I dream often and plan a lot. But I do that planning during intentional morning planning sessions. There is living, and there is planning. Waking up means knowing the difference and keeping them separate.

To be more present, playful and peaceful, we must learn to stay awake and listen to our needs; pay attention to our wants; and focus on what makes us happy inside. And when we do that, we naturally learn to slow down and focus on this moment, right here. As we work with this habit of staying awake, it's important to start where we might need the most work — in our ears, in what we hear and how we listen to the pulse of our family and those around us — including our own needs.

Savoring Slow Invitation: Start listening more now to what your family needs — as if you are listening to your family's heartbeat. Just listen. When a thought or a need arises, make a note of it in a tiny journal somewhere. Your list might be simple, like "we need to eat more fruits and vegetables," or it might be more complicated, such as "we need to talk to a professional." Knowing is the first step. So just listen so you will know more.

Waking up to the magic of the everyday

There is this belief system ingrained in us that we have to be somewhere special or be doing something special to feel like we're having a great day. Those ordinary moments we find ourselves in all week long, however, are just as magical.

We don't need big holidays or sparkling decorations. We don't need to decorate our homes like those in a Pottery Barn catalog. We don't have to have the best crafts to show off.

None of this is where magic is found. Abundance doesn't live in things. It lives in our hearts.

Magic is the way our children's legs and their little bodies naturally fold around our own and fit perfectly during a Saturday afternoon nap.

Magic is the way you glide easily in and out of conversations that range from what's for dinner to how a booger is gross to please go wash your hands, all while waiting for the peas to cook.

Magic is the way we stoop down real close just to smell that mix of part dirt and part baby that still lingers on their necks.

Magic is the way we sit down and give up the to-do list to read a poem, to smile and nod about a love note they've given us or just to stop and listen to a long, detailed and confusing story.

Magic is the smile we offer each day, even when we might not feel like smiling.

Magic is the wonder and curiosity that lives in their eyes each day they wake up. If we look around today, we'll see magic everywhere we go. Imagine the abundance of simply opening our eyes and paying attention. These moments might be WOW moments. They might be a-ha! moments, too. But, mostly, they are just ... well, magical.

I've walked through my days half asleep, barely paying attention to what surrounds me.

And I've walked through my days awake, noticing everything and being surprised and in awe of the simplest things.

The times I spend awake and paying attention to the tiniest of details are by far my favorite moments. Once you learn to live in a state of wow, everything is beautiful.

In fact, paying attention and being in the moment is really the only way I know how to slow time.

In her book "Mitten Strings for God: Reflections for Mothers in a Hurry," author Katrina Kenison wrote about these dailyness moments with ease.

"If my experience as a mother has taught me anything, it is to be awake for such moments, to keep life simple enough to allow them to occur, and to appreciate their fleeting beauty ..."

That is what it means to wake up.

Waking up is a habit you can practice over and over again until you get it right.(Tweet this!)

In fact, it's a habit that's constantly a work in progress, as more and more distractions work their way into our busy lives.

You might find yourself mostly awake on some days. Or

perhaps just three times in a day. And some days, you might not be awake much at all.

The point is not in the numbers. The point is in the trying. The practice of waking up is a lifelong love affair you can continue forever.

All we're trying to do is elevate the ordinary by seeing all the beauty and all the imperfections in a single moment in time. It might be just a matter of staring lovingly at those who are around us and who demonstrate their love to us each day.

It's about celebrating the little charming rays of sunshine that grace our days and our nights and all the in betweens.

It's about embracing all that surrounds us — like little love notes, the way someone holds our face with compassion, and friends who just get us like no one else ever will.

It's about devoting our full presence to the mundane and the common, and trying to crack open the beauty of it so we can remember it forever.

It's about celebrating that ordinary moment when we find ourselves lost and dizzy with happiness.

Savoring Slow Invitation: Take an ordinary moment and search for what makes it extraordinary. Whisper what you are grateful for right now. Make a list of all the magic that unfolds right before you, right there under your own eye lids — and in between each amazing breath.

Waking up and finding ordinary bliss

Those moments, the ones that stop time for a little bit, can be fleeting.

We blink, we spend too much time cleaning, and we miss them.

We all need gentle nudges to remind us to remember to stop and enjoy the little things.

The hugs. The kisses. The spontaneous game of Frisbee or injuring yourself doing a cartwheel when you have no business doing a cartwheel. It's about standing in a secret location, watching imaginary play unfold because your child has suddenly become a little self-conscious that she's being watched and will freeze up when she knows you're watching.

Waking up is a habit about making life more beautiful and more meaningful. It's about adding sparkle and bling to the everyday routine we find ourselves knee-deep in day after day.

It's about how good the sheets feel after you change them on a Sunday afternoon and about how wonderful a room feels when it's picked up and the blinds are open wide.

It's about the smell of the deep woods during a hike. Or feeling the warmth of holding someone's hand. Or following a little child's passionate lead to nowhere, or rushing to see a big bug you didn't want to see or feeling cool creek water running through your fingers. Or spontaneous teddy bear picnics in the backyard.

When you find yourself drifting away and feeling more distracted, stop and remind yourself to wake up and notice the beauty.

Notice the Beauty Meditation

When you wake today, may you notice.

May you pay attention.

May you see and honor the tiny, yet beautiful details of life unfolding before your very eyes. May you feel how the earth holds you up, grounds you and gives you something to stand on, something to stand for each day. May you smell the coffee as it gradually drifts from room to room. May you breathe in the morning air, the smells of new beginnings, of starting overs, of delicious conspiracies you can turn into your reality.

May you see your partner. How he or she follows the same routine. How he or she takes time to notice the little things. May You hear what is not only said but meant. May You be open to that love between you.

And when the children wake early, long before the sun rises, may you Notice.

May you pay attention. May you realize this, too, will most definitely pass.

May you laugh as their bed heads make their hair do twisty, weird things. May you feel how their warmth radiates from their hearts, filling yours. Smell their sweetness and innocence before everyone gets too busy to gather close again. Notice what their eyes are drawn to out of curiosity and wonder.

May you notice what inspires them to smile. May you smile with them at the beauty of everything.

As you go about your day, and your family goes about theirs, May You Pay attention to the birds singing outside your windows. May you notice the way the green stems are peeking up through the ground. May you notice how the clouds are billowing away their time in the sky, traveling, floating.

May you notice the way all the people you pass are just human beings, fighting to survive another day themselves. May you notice how they warm your heart even if they are strangers, even if they are not like you.

And when you come back together as a family, May you pay attention to what isn't said at all. May you look into each others' eyes and notice how bright they are, or tired they are, or excited they are. May you cook slowly, eat slowly and linger longer together, just relishing your meal for what it is — sustenance, soul food, nourishment. May you savor that food and the memories of eating together. May you notice that this moment is what matters.

May you pay attention to the joy that crosses their faces as you say YES, finally, again, once more. May you notice how that makes you feel, to make people happy because you can, because you wanted to and because you could.

As your day comes to an end, May you notice how the light fades in each of your rooms. How the energy rises .... rises .... rises and then watch it as it falls, comes to a sleepy end. May you notice how little bodies shiver and lips turn blue as they dry off from their bath. May you notice how the knots have gotten more tangled as their hair has grown, as they have grown. May you notice that the line on the bathroom wall where you last measured is far below where their head would be now.

May you notice that life is right here, this moment and no other. May you notice that you just survived a day without tackling your to-do list. May you notice that you, too, have needs. A bath. A good book. A sweet wine. A massage. A long night's sleep. To talk to a friend. To write long and full of run-on sentences because you have so much to express, so much to say and there aren't enough hours to remember it all, even though you really wish you could so you just have to write them down before you forget the beauty.

May you pay attention to all that matters today. And nothing more.

Savoring Slow Invitation: As you go about your day, start noticing the way the light hits just the right way on everything you see. Start smelling the way a room smells or the way your child's hair or neck smells. Start paying attention to the warmth or the chill in the air and how it feels on your skin. Noticing the details is the most beautiful way to walk in this world.

Waking up to your child's childhood

One early morning, as a light layer of fog lifted from the earth, my daughter asked for a cup of hot tea in a mug she could take outside.

She grabbed her tea and went tip-toeing outside onto our patio.

She sat down, wrapped her arms around her knees, tucked into her chest, and watched the world around her. She didn't do anything else. She just sat and enjoyed the moment.

I was amazed at how she drank her tea and took in the happenings of the busy backyard. She craned her neck to watch an airplane. She closed her eyes and listened for birds. She watched as neighbors' dogs walked along.

"She's growing up," I thought.

We're afraid we're going to miss our children when they are grown up, and yet we create such busy lives — doing so many other things — we forget to simply stop and watch them grow up.

You can do that. You can watch them. And notice them. And stare at them.

It's a meditation in and of itself and a wonderful way to build a habit of waking up.

I've done a lot of staring at my children.

When they are in the zone of being a kind, happy child, I could stare at them for a long, long time.

I love seeing the mystery of who they are becoming start to reveal itself. I love seeing their experimentations of who they want to be rise to the surface. I love witnessing tiny sparks of their humanness.

Here are a few ways to really notice your child:

1. **Stare at them.** As our babies turn to toddlers who turn to big kids who can do it all by themselves, it's so easy to stop looking at them with that same loving gaze we gave them when they were doing so many firsts — first sit up, first smile, first crawl, first steps. Now that they have mastered many things, the firsts are fleeting. All the more to pay attention to them when they happen. Notice their beauty. First braids. First time doing each other's hair. Noted.

2. **Listen to them.** My daughters have never had to get my attention by saying Mommy, Mommy, Mommy, Mommy. But that doesn't mean I'm always the best listener. This week I have been hearing my children's thoughts in a much deeper way. I've let their words roll through my mind. I've repeated what they've said back to me. I've been impressed with their use of words, like "literally," which was used incorrectly, but with the best intentions. My goodness, such big words for such little girls, I keep thinking. When did they get such a mature vocabulary?

3. **Go with their flow.** At the silent retreat, our theme of the

day was flowing water. Children are the river. We try to be those rocks and dams built up along the path of the river but the water just glides right over us. We cannot control the way it flows. We cannot control how it expands with the seasons. I like to watch my children's seasons unfold. What patterns are you noticing in your child's life?

4. **What do they love?** In our house, we call it filling our buckets. We, as parents, often know what makes us happy. But what about our children? What brings those amazing smiles to their faces? If you pay enough attention, you will figure it out.

5. **Write it down.** By taking time to reflect on each of our children each day, we are noticing the good in our days together. And it also offers a great little pile of memories to sit back and read once they are grown and out on their own.

Savoring Slow Invitation: Take some time today to just watch your child in action. Really be there in that moment with him as he's building or digging or playing that game. This insight might tell you something you've been missing on how to connect and relate. This form of noticing and meditation is going to open you up to what matters.

Waking up to the abundance of the in-between moments
The knot in her necklace chain was small and tight.

The bus was on its way. Time was ticking. My internal mama alarm clock was going off.

But on the other side of that knot was a face filled with beautiful little girl anticipation.

The look of love was already forming on her face for me pulling this off as if she knew more than I did.

There wasn't any time. And yet there was plenty of time.

It seemed hopeless.

And yet everything inside of me told me to not put this one off, to not brush this moment aside.

Slow down and Ban Busy when everything around you says speed up but your heart says stop.

In this moment, I pushed snooze on my internal mama alarm clock.

Maybe I pushed it twice.

My fingers worked that knot slowly yet patiently. Beads of sweat formed on my upper lip.

I looked up to see her big hazel eyes, waiting.

And when it finally untangled and was set free, we embraced.

Because when kindness comes before timeliness, all of life is worth a big hug.

She rushed off to catch the bus.

This is how I slow time in my own home — by surrendering to those moments in between. This is how I untangle my own hours.

Savoring Slow Invitation: This week, take time and just notice how you spend your time — all the knots you spend untangling and all the imaginary set ups you spend undoing. And consider that on the other side of those moments, there is most likely a face or two waiting in anticipation, filled with hope that you will be there for them. Catch yourself if you are rushing through these small yet amazing moments of connection with those you love.

Savoring Slow Habit No. 2 | Release

_____

"Always say 'yes' to the present moment. What could be more futile, more insane, than to create inner resistance to what already is? What could be more insane than to oppose life itself, which is now and always now? Surrender to what is. Say 'yes' to life — and see how life suddenly starts working for you rather than against you." ~ Eckhart Tolle

***

What would happen if just today you let go of the tight grip you keep on your life?

Would the world fall apart?

Would YOUR world fall apart?

What if you didn't care about what your children ate, the activities they did, if your partner packed their lunch or even if they were going to be home late again?

Will the sun still come up tomorrow? Will your family still be OK?

What if, just for today, you didn't care what other people

thought, and you just did your own thing without worry or societal pressures?

Would all that authenticity make you shine brighter?

What if all those balls you're juggling in the air just fell one by one onto the ground and shattered on the floor?

Would you be upset, or would you be relieved?

How would it feel to just be, without trying to get to the next best thing?

Would everything you have right now, this very second, be enough?

What if you just stopped caring so much about life's minutiae and started paying attention to all the beauty that surrounds you instead? Who cares if you really say no to volunteering, just this once? Who cares if you really say yes to skipping the latest social event, just this once?

Especially if it means more time to yourself? Or more time with your family?

The image of releasing my tight grip on all the many things I try to control all day is a beautiful, profound thought — and absolutely terrifying at times.

If this is hard for you, too, then understand you are not alone. Releasing is our second habit to work on to create less busyness in our world.

What can you release today? Beds not getting made? An unkept house? Piles of laundry? Children squabbling in the other room? If they ate iced Pop-Tarts over the new box of organic shredded wheat? If their clothes match? Finding the perfect photo to share on your blog or on Facebook or to send across the miles?

That everything is perfectly imperfect?

When we release, we let go of tasks that are holding power over our energy.

To release simply means choosing something else that feels better.

This habit is as much about celebrating as it is about feeling lighter. Imagine yourself holding on to a really strong balloon. Something that is causing you stress. And then you let it go and release it from your life. You are instantly lighter.

> Savoring Slow Invitation: Write a list of all the things you have to do today. I mean truly have to do today. Now, circle only the ones that are life or death — meaning they have to be done today or someone gets hurt. What's left?

Learning to let it be

And when the broken-hearted people
  Living in the world agree
  There will be an answer
  Let it be. – The Beatles

We hang on tight to a lot of things.
That awful vase your mother-in-law gave you.
The huge pearl ring your aunt said she wanted you to have.
Names we call ourselves that aren't very nice.

Drama at work or in the PTO.

The news.

Politics and social issues also seem to inspire good people to lose their minds.

When we choose to let something be we choose to not take up our time and energy thinking about it.

If you want to live a life that is about Savoring Slow you have to start doing some things differently.

Savoring Slow Invitation: What would you like to let go of this month? Maybe a long-held belief, an insecurity, a personality trait? Perhaps you need to let go of a worry or fear or an area in your life you are trying to perfect? Or, perhaps you need to let go of an obligation that just doesn't feel right? Now, take the steps to let it go.

Learning to let go.

Letting go and releasing the things troubling us is not easy. And yet we know what we need to do. We need to let go. We need to release the negative energy to feel lighter and more peaceful.

So let go.

Let go of the worries and the imaginary tragedies that unfold in your mind — and just breathe.

Let go of the concept of easy — nothing is.

Let go of wanting to keep things just as they are — be open to what happens next.

Let go of what you want — and be happy with what you have.

Let go of who's letting you down — and start focusing on who's building you up.

Let go of what you thought your life was going to be like — and embrace how it has turned out with a great big YES!

Let go of every single notion that you are less than, imperfect, not good enough — and accept yourself, finally.

Let go of how the story was supposed to end — and trust that this is just the beginning.

Let go of hoping for the ideal — and become best friends with what it means to be content.

And when it's not that easy, I offer you these tips to let go:

1. Breathing — Just a single deep breath can slow you down to release the tension.

2. Feeling — Notice your feelings. Name them. Understand your emotions on a deeper level because they are yours and they mean something important. So when you are feeling frustrated, say the words, "I am frustrated." This is how we can better communicate with ourselves and those around us.

3. Declaring — My favorite way to let go is by using a short statement or mantra. Some of my favorites are "It is what it is." "Let go." Or the popular "This too shall pass."

4. Give Thanks — Simply naming one GOOD to COUNTER one negative feeling or experience is a quick boost to letting go.

5. Self-care — Take one small step toward happy for YOU. Go to another room and put on a happy song. Put on a cup of tea. Eat a piece of dark chocolate. Write a list. Take a photo. Take a walk.

Savoring Slow Invitation — For today, write a list of all the things you are clinging really tightly to in your life. Things you don't want to change. People or situations you don't want to change. Or perhaps situations you do want to change and you're doing everything you can to change it and not seeing progress. All of these things you are clinging to is your list of mental work and that mental work is keeping you very busy. For today, just write the list. Don't do anything else with the list.

Words to let go from your vocabulary right now

BUSY

I've never posted on Facebook — or any other social media — that I'm really busy just as an everyday sort of update.

Busy is not the story I want to tell people.

Recent research tells us that we're all obsessed with being busy. In fact, on social media, there's almost a competition about who is the busiest. Families with children are, perhaps, the busiest of all, but that doesn't mean we have to say as much.

So what do you say instead? The answer to this question will become more clear by the end of this book. For now, focus on just how many times you are using the word without thought and start finding ways to change your story.

Begin with loving what you do every day. For instance, I love meal planning. It's tedious and it's taken me years to perfect, but I truly enjoy it. When you love something, it doesn't make you feel busy. My husband loves to the mow the grass. I have often suggested that he hire someone to mow since he commutes two and a half hours a day. But that time is meditative for him and is a nice break from his ordinary routine, so he insists on doing it himself.

For a long, long time I hated to do the dishes. In the last year, though, I've even managed to change that story and make doing the dishes an experience that I enjoy. A fresh washcloth. Some music. A candle. Looking out the window. Followed by some lotion on my hands. It really can be a slow, beautiful moment.

Living life is the story I choose to tell. So I will share all the cool things we did that day even if the coolest thing was planting seeds in a garden.

It's time to change your busy story.

What are you so busy doing, anyway?

SHOULD

Perhaps it's just me, but I have a pretty big aversion to the word should.

Growing up, I was told I should do a lot of things, and I always questioned all of those things (after doing most of them, of course).

If the shoulds of our life come from within — and they are real and raw and honest, such as I should take a shower or I should clean the bathtub — then it is clear why you should listen to the should. But if the shoulds are ringing in your ears about what another person (or group) might think of you if you don't do that should, then perhaps it's time to evaluate your attachment to that should.

There are many shoulds that come with a price if we don't do them. Not going to that school fundraiser. Not going to that big event in town that everyone's been talking about. Not going to that evening work event that is optional just to look good to your boss. Appearances and assumptions really can — and will — influence how we spend our days, our hours, without even really thinking about it.

As soon as you start banning the word should — or at least double checking yourself when you use it — you will reclaim that feeling of power over your hours that instantly frees up extra time for doing what you love.

COULD

As the sneaky, bratty cousin of the word SHOULD, this word is something to watch out for as you work toward a slower life.

The coulds sneak up on you, especially when you are in a slow, easygoing mood.

These coulds disguise themselves as opportunities to belong, to fit in, to feel needed, to be helpful and to feel worthy. For example, maybe this sounds familiar: "Sure, I could help you tomorrow." The fundraiser. The special birthday party. The new project at work that just happens to be on the weekend of next week.

All of these coulds really add up, so it's important to think before you say yes. Think before you jump in with both feet and promise something to someone you may not want to deliver on later. Yes, you could, but you may not feel happy doing it and then you are stuck.

Avoiding the could domino effect is important so that you don't face guilt and shame later. Knowing what works for you now and how it will flow into your future time and space is important.

Whenever I feel ready to act, I like to say this mantra: Just because I can, doesn't mean I should.

And that's my final offering to you on this topic.

Just because I can, doesn't mean I should.

BORED

As much as we all long for a slow life, we must understand that with that can come a feeling of boredom.

When you take away all of that rushing, you're left with quiet time with your thoughts.

Last year, when I decided to quit my 9-to-5 job and become a full-time blogger and business owner, I was suddenly faced with hours of alone time. Big emotions started to arise, and I was finding myself stirring up old emotions.

Same goes for your family. Your children will likely say that a slow day at home is boring. Of course, their threshold for fun is much higher than any of us can ever actually meet.

By letting go of the word bored, we're instantly challenged to be more creative and interesting, naturally. A slow day at our house recently included creating our own board games, family art projects, slow walks and interviewing each other.

At our house, the words can't and bored are just not allowed. We'll talk more about boredom and how to cope with it later in this book.

GUILT

Right now, as I write this, I'm staring at a pile of papers on the counter and a kitchen floor that is half-covered with things that just shouldn't be there.

And today, instead of writing all day, I'll be hanging with my kids for their first of four days off from school.

Normally, I'd use this as a great day to clean, for once.

But I'm not going to do that today. And I'm not going to feel guilty for not doing it either.

Picking up will happen as the day progresses. We're not going to live like slobs. The kids will have to take their two pairs of roller skates down to the basement, for instance. And the box and wrapping paper from a relative's gift will get put in the trash.

The rest? It can wait.

Because on a day like today, when we get to be together and enjoy each other's company all day, that's what I want to do. I don't smother my kids, though, so there will be time and space when they will be reading or playing and I'll have the time I need to keep things in order.

Guilt over what we should — I mean ought — to do is a powerful guide over our days and our hours. We let guilt rule the house rather than our hearts.

FEAR

We carry this fear inside us that we're going to fail our children.

I feel it right now because they haven't been in any organized activities for about six months.

Forget the fact that they are happy and thriving, building forts outside and playing school inside.

Forget the fact that they are growing fine and learning great and laughing all the time.

I'm the worst mother ever for not putting them into a sport or an activity.

That's what I tell myself.

This fear, though, is my own making.

We fill our schedules up out of fear. And then we wish we weren't so busy because we think — we know — a slower pace is what we need as a family.

I have a client in my coaching practice who literally spends her weekends running herself crazy because she's afraid her son will just want to watch TV at home. And that puts her in fear mode. So she intentionally creates a really busy day outside of the house to avoid that screen-time fear.

The words afraid, fear, terrified ... these are our vocabulary because we don't know any other way. We haven't been here before — with so many options and so little time.

And so I go back to the single most important questions I ever ask myself — or my children.

What do we want to do?

What feels right to us?

What's most important right now?

And usually after I go through those questions, I know what needs to be done.

And sometimes what needs to be done is signing up for violin lessons.

And sometimes what needs to be done is dropping out of gymnastics lessons.

You just never know until you ask yourself.

So ask.

And then listen.

And be ready to act and make changes.

Savoring Slow Invitation — Think about all the things you do each day/week/month/year and consider what is no longer serving you or your family well. What can you release? What no longer feels really good and is starting to feel more like a burden. Write a good-bye letter to that "thing," whatever it is, explaining to it why you no longer need it in your life.

Savoring Slow Habit No. 3 | Reframe

"For fast-acting relief, slow down," — Lily Tomlin

***

For the longest time, I thought I suffered from a lack of time.

There were never enough hours in the day to do it all — the laundry, the dishes, the meals, taking care of myself — and the kids — taking care of the house and nurturing my own dreams. Not to mention our marriage.

And then I realized one day in the middle of it all that perhaps I don't have to do it all.

Perhaps I can release some of these things right now and lose that sense of urgency that seems to invade my mind at certain times in the year.

Life is going to be busy as long as we want to be a part of it.

Our job then, it seems, is very clear: Make time our best friend forever and surrender to the ease that a slower pace can bring. By making peace with the clock — and all that you have to do — you can instantly feel like you have more time.

As we consider this next habit — reframe — we must consider the stories we've been telling ourselves for years about how we spend our time and how we wish to spend our time. This Savoring Slow habit is going to help you break the habit of saying you're busy by helping you reframe your busy story.

One of my favorite days last summer began after a long morning of hiking and swimming, but in the back of my mind I knew I had a million things to do: blog posts to write, social media to schedule, dinner to prep, rooms to pick up and tidy and, not to mention, taking care of my own needs.

But as I looked at the clock I realized I still had eight hours left in our day before the kids went to sleep.

That afternoon, once the rain took over the sky, I laid down on the couch and called one of my girls to me. She flopped her 7-year-old body down, surrendering on top of me. Within minutes, she was asleep, breathing loudly and deeply. She drooled on my shoulder. She stirred a bit.

I wondered if her type of sleep is why she wakes so frequently at night and I felt a pang of guilt for not listening more to what she sounds like when she sleeps.

I couldn't remember the last time she'd done that, fell asleep on her mommy. When she was a baby, I guess. I admit, I loved every hot, sweaty second of it.

Soon, her sister joined us, trying to find a space to nestle in to our mound and, once settled, was fast asleep as well, something she's done more frequently with me as her body pillow.

Sometimes, if I'm really patient, ease is letting go of all that I think I'm supposed to be and just surrendering to who I am right now, at this very minute.

Savoring Slow Invitation: What is the busy story you've been telling yourself and others? Think about how you have viewed your full life to this point. Is it good busy? If so, start thinking about how you can reframe this story to make it feel like you have more control of your days.

What about all that housework?

I know I've thought the following statements many times in my own life.

If we could just hurry up and get our chores done, we will finally have some time to relax and play.

If the house is clean, I can finally feel happy.

This is the busy trap. This is the idea that we can't be happy unless we're doing something, and everything is perfect.

Except most of us are having a hard time reaching that enlightened state of blissful perfection.

Routines, being organized and having enough family time are always looming in the back and front of our minds because those things do have to get done, but they aren't what we prefer to do.

"Where can I find balance?" moms ask me all the time.

We often forget there is a middle ground. A place of contentment without too much stress.

Surrendering to what needs to be done and not resisting it is the first step.

And, yes, a clean, organized house is often more peaceful, more creative and more joyful but sometimes what is needed most — a nap, for instance — is the quickest path to reaching it.

We can enjoy our lives — all parts of it —without rushing through it. We can start to find ways to appreciate the parts of the day that help create that loving, kind household we dream about.

To reframe means to shift your thinking

John Robinson, well-known as Father Time, is the leading sociologist who studies time use.

Robinson has said repeatedly that one of the best ways to feel less busy is actually not to take more vacations or even do less but, rather, to simply stop saying you're so busy.

I agree, but I'd like to take that a step further and show you that your time is valuable and everything you're doing is important. Yes, you are busy, but you're busy doing things you love. And, if you're not, it's time to make a few changes.

But let's start with reframing how we look at our busy lives. Let's reframe — and rework — our to-do lists.

Let's start asking, "What does busy really mean?"

Does it mean a burdened life?

Or does it mean a full life?

Does it mean chaos?

Or does it mean opportunity?

The next few sections will help you reach a place of surrender with your busy life and your ordinary routine as well as help you surrender to those moments that happen every day, maybe twice a day, maybe three times a day.

Meals. Diaper changes. Weeding. Watering. Kissing boo-boos. Picking up toys. Folding and hanging towels that were left on the floor.

It's all important. But maybe after that quick nap on the couch with a baby drooling on your shoulder.

Make time your friend

There is a way to start understanding your own idea of time and seeing if there is anything you can do to create a better relationship with the clock and the to-do lists.

Just like tracking how much money you spend is good for budgeting, tracking how you are spending your hours is also a great way to understand where your time is going.

When I began logging my time each day, my eyes were opened to many things, and I am not talking about the time I wasted — though, there was plenty of that, to be honest.

The surprising part was how much I accomplished. How much I was fitting in. How much living I was doing — and, as a result, my children were doing.

And then I quickly realized how my time is spent on weird things like plucking my eye brows and fixing the shower curtain rings that always fall off while opening and closing the curtain.

There is no book for how to deal with the little itty bitty time stealers. We must learn to savor every moment because every moment is our life.

Taking that step back to see the bigger picture of our days gives us permission to release some of our "we have to get this done" expectations I carried around and allowed for more goofing off.

How do you want to spend your time?

The first step is to ask yourself a real question.

How do I want to spend my time?

If you could change the pattern of your day to make more space and time for things, what would you choose? More time to play with your kids? More time for your own self-care? More time for baking?

How you spend your time is in your control. Seize every moment as if it's your last.

And then start tracking and logging your time. It's not as simple as it sounds because, when you're so busy doing it, it can be hard to add in one more thing. But you can look back at everything you did, that will be enough.

But if you want more detailed data on how you are spending your time, you can keep a detailed log in all the rooms you spend the most time. Your office. The family computer. The kitchen. Even take one in the car with you for errands and appointments.

The idea is not to feel bad about how you are spending your time, but to actually feel better about your time. You may realize that playing that computer game is actually just a symptom of being tired and worn out and that what you really need is just a good night's sleep or a good walk around the block.

Savoring Slow Invitation: Now that you have the family on board, released what is not working and begun to reframe your own schedule and idea of time, what are you noticing as you track your time? What is your schedule feeling like? Are you seeing any shifts in what you are saying yes to or no to now? Are you making any new discoveries about how you want to spend your time versus how you are supposed to spend your time?

Going with the flow of your days

"Don't try to steer the river," says Deepak Chopra.

"When I let go of what I am, I become what I might be," says Lao Tzu.

Better than both of those quotes is this one:

"It is not action or effort that we must surrender; it is self-will, and this is terribly difficult. You must do your best constantly, yet never allow yourself to become involved in whether things work out the way you want." ~ Eknath Easwaran

My daughters' rivers are always flowing in new and unpredictable directions, and I can't do a thing about it. They have changed too much. Things that used to excite them no longer grab their interest.

Instead of playing a game with me after dinner, they want to wrestle with each other.

Instead of arts and crafts, they want to do cartwheels and backbends and play leap frog.

Instead of helping me in the kitchen, they want me to call them when it's ready.

The river they follow is the only one they know, the only one they can follow. I can only float beside them, bobbing along with the many twists and turns that are ahead of us.

And, strangely, I am at peace with this.

What can often feel so scary about slow, unplanned days is the uncertainty of what it will bring to a family.

Busyness keeps us distracted and moving forward.

Standing still, however, can create friction.

It's often easier to just keep moving and doing, but that is also what can create that overwhelmed, burned-out feeling we can carry around all day.

But when we start to reframe what slow means — not bored, just moving at a slower pace — you start to understand how a slow schedule can really work for your family, and you start to see those slow days not as a burden but as an opportunity to wander, wonder, create and connect.

These "go with the flow" days always lead us back to a deeper connection.

For my family, to contain the craziness that can easily take over, we keep these slow rules in mind when planning out a week or the month:

- One family activity per day. This is the daily stuff that pops up. Going to the library, the store, a relative's house. These are ordinary things that happen, but they don't all have to happen in one day.

- One big activity per weekend. This is the bigger life things that add to our day. A family hike and a picnic, going to the movies, attending a social event.

- One really big adventure per month. This includes day trips, going to museums, and other really fun things that are often rather costly.

We alternate busy with calm and quiet with active. This means our days together follow a flow, as much as possible, that involves weaving calm moments in between our busy moments all day. We often wake up and are in a calm state and so by mid morning, we're ready to move into more active or busy activities.

Now and then, busy days or weeks happen, so these rules are

meant to be broken when bigger and more exciting things happen in life. When you go with the flow, you are more able to handle the really crazy weeks that are bound to happen, especially if you have school-age kids.

The benefits of keeping a schedule in order to have slower days is that you get to decide what and when you will do things rather than feeling obligated and torn. You can say yes to that spontaneous dinner invitation with friends instead of saying you'll have to pass because your schedule is too full.

Savoring Slow Invitation: Start looking at your schedule in terms of busy and non-busy moments. See if you can find a way to start balancing those more evenly during the week and month. See if you can really find a flow that allows for busy and non-busy activities.

Here are some ways to follow your own family's flow.

- Study it. Before you implement a new schedule or a change in the rules, study what is currently happening. What is the natural flow and order of things now? If you change that, is it worth the stresses that may come with it?

- Let go. Perhaps dinnertime hasn't been working out. The kids are crying. You can't seem to find the time you need to make the food. What would happen if you surrendered and let go? Just toss together some cheese, bread, fruit and veggies? Stop trying to force anything at all. Forget your agenda and release your idea of normal for a single day.

- **Lower your expectations.** It can be hard for us to give up the expectations we have created for our families. When the day fails, or looks like it could fail, we can feel cranky. Often, the best days are the ones where we have no set agenda and just go along with whatever happens.

- **Go with the flow.** Ride the river. Things will get done, maybe not on your rigid timeline but they will get done. It's better not to fight the flow that your children are in right now. Find natural moments to work in good conversations, reading aloud and teachable moments. Find natural moments to play together and work together to tackle the chores. Parenting is a lot like waiting for the right time to step onto the down escalator. Timing is absolutely everything for a smooth ride. And once you're on, you feel relieved.

- **Accept imperfection.** Some days just don't turn out the way you want them to. Some days you're just picking up the pieces of the chaos. That's motherhood. That's parenthood. That's life with children. Embrace your mistakes and everyone's mistakes around you. Accept that sometimes we need to make mistakes in order to learn valuable new lessons.

- **Keep perspective.** The flow of a day with children is not always perfect, but it's always open and ripe with possibilities. Children, if we allow them, can lead us to laughter and smiles. Silly dances and awful jokes. Their version of the world is so much more vivid and interesting than our own. Keeping this in perspective is always a great way to move with ease in the flow of your day.

Slow down your expectations

Sometimes life with children feels like a constant uphill battle for more time.

That if we don't accomplish everything right now it will never get done.

This feeling of time slipping away and never getting it back is often the cause of our sense of urgency to hurry and get things done right now, this second. Because of that fear of never accomplishing everything we want to accomplish, we live in a constant state of hurry up.

After all, we have a vision in our head of what our life is supposed to be like and look like. How are we going to achieve that vision if we don't hurry?

Except we already have a life that is real and perfectly imperfect as it is, and we're seriously rushing through it.

Time is passing by quickly but perhaps not as quickly as we think it is in our minds.

Our minds play really great games with our thoughts.

If I've learned anything, it's not to trust our minds, in fact.

Being ready to tackle those thoughts that arise that say hurry up, rush along now or go fast is a valuable skill in slowing down your day — without actually changing a single thing.

For me, using positive statements like mantras and intentions really help me feel less hurried.

Savoring Slow Invitation: Start intentionally using positive statements to experience slower days. Instead of starting out with bouts of dread and stress about what you have to do, find new ways to tell your story with a joyful, positive spin.

Savoring Slow Intentions

- Today, may I feel at ease with all the imperfections that unfold around me. May today feel perfectly imperfect.

- Today, may I feel a release of fully letting go of those things I cannot change. May today feel lighter and more joyful as a result.

- Today, may I feel happy and joyful no matter what happens. May today be full of little surprises simply because I am paying attention to all that is around me.

- Today, may my mind and body remain calm and relaxed. May today feel like all that matters is loving people for who they are right now.

Savoring Slow Mantras

- Go slowly.
- Take the slow path.

- Take it all in.

- There is no rush.

- Focus on what matters.

- Notice the details.

- Be inspired.

- Be here now.

Savoring Slow Affirmations

- By intentionally choosing to slow down and live with purpose, I am opening my heart up to wonderful new experiences and all the beauty in this world.

- Moving slowly I walk with my feet firmly planted on the earth, one step at a time, moving closer and closer to my connection with the Universe and all the beings I come in contact with.

- When I choose to slow down and start savoring slow, my breathing instantly gets deeper and my lungs fuller. My head spins with a bit of happy dizziness, and I start to remember what it feels like to be fully alive and awake.

Savoring Slow Habit No. 4 | Focus

"Doing nothing is better than being busy doing nothing" — Lao Tzu

***

When my daughters were 10 months old, I quit my job as the director of a teen mother mentorship program and stayed home to be a freelance writer.

As a former newsroom journalist, I had the skills.

What I didn't have was the time.

Writing happened when the babies were sleeping for their morning and afternoon naps.

I had a good system. I would put out the calls to sources in the morning. And I'd field the calls in the afternoon.

That usually worked out pretty well.

But on this one particular day I was on a tight deadline for a newspaper profile of an esteemed businessman in another state. I needed to speak with him. And I needed to take his call whenever his busy schedule would allow for it.

You know, because he was a very busy man.

So, while my two babies were sitting in their highchairs eating pureed sweet potatoes, the phone rang. And I needed to take that call.

And so I did.

I fed the babies. Asked the busy man all the questions I needed to ask. I wrote down his answers in my reporter's notebook. And I did it all while making sure to entertain the kiddos in silence dance moves because what busy businessman wants to hear two babies crying?

This was the epitome of multitasking.

It wasn't long after that, though, when I realized I didn't need to do it all.

And I started to work harder at being mindful and in the moment. The practice of zen is not easy, and so it's always a practice in motion in my own life. Right now, as I write this book, I am practicing zen because I am doing this and only this.

Does this mean my to-do list isn't important? Or that social media isn't notifying me of new messages?

No. It just means that right now this is my priority. And when I close my laptop and decide what is next on my list, I will do that one thing, and so on and so on. And, honestly, we can only do one thing at a time despite what we tell ourselves.

There is no greater pleasure than feeling on top of the world because you're on top of the to-do list.

Unfortunately, these moments are often fleeting as our growing lists of demands, responsibilities and adult agendas keep us spinning.

And our list of wants, desires and dreams keep us rushing through our list of to-dos.

As it turns out, though, multitasking is really just polluting our time. It steals away our ability to enjoy the moment and live in the present.

It's actually messing with our heads and making us feel like you don't have enough time for anything.

Why is time contamination so wrong?

Actually, multitasking is not wrong. We've been successful and accomplished in our lives doing multiple things at once — or so we think.

There are many good reasons to eat your lunch at the computer while taking a phone call. Or while nursing a baby and surfing the Internet.

These things keep the day flowing.

Why time contamination is so wrong to our mission of Savoring Slow, though, is another issue all together.

We cannot savor the beauty and the wonder in the world when we are so busy trying to remember where we were in a conversation we just left to do something else. We cannot stop to notice the details or smell the peonies or watch a worm if all of our senses are tied up with three other tasks that we're trying to rush through so we can have more time later.

Savoring Slow is about avoiding time contamination most of the time. It's about beautiful, slow living — one moment at a time. It's about a wide open heart and mind while accomplishing what is most important right this moment (which, by the way, is always the safety of your child).

How to live more mindfully

There are so many experts on mindfulness. And I suspect, it will continue to grow as the number of distractions in our lives grow. And, yes, meditation does work, but there are so many of us with children underfoot all day long there's not much time for sitting in quiet trying not to think.

In fact, many of my attempts to meditate even first thing in the morning have been interrupted. And this book is about living a mindful, intentional life all day long without ever actually sitting down on a meditation cushion.

So I want to share what I do to bring myself back to being focused on one thing and one thing only.

Talking to myself.

Seriously.

I first talk to myself in the morning when I set my daily intention for how I want the day to flow. And then I step right into my life armed with mantras I can repeat over and over again until I get it right. And when I'm failing in all of this, I use positive statements to bring me back to center and try again.

Through this self-talk, I am able to stay in the moment longer and more frequently and also to intentionally limit the number of distractions I allow myself to get influenced by in single day. These statements are meant to be lived as much as they are stated in your head.

Savoring Slow Invitation: Start using slow mantras in your daily life. Stay open to the idea that your habits of multi-tasking and doing too much can be changed.

The Do One Thing or Do Nothing Mantra

Once you see the value in putting all of yourself into a moment or a single task — uni-tasking — it's easy to return to it again and again.

This applies to everything. Do one thing or do nothing simply means if you can't put all of your effort into something, then don't do it.

Do one thing that is big that week.

Do one activity per day, per week, per month.

The power of one is incredible when you make it an intentional choice.

This rule is pretty simple. When I'm with my kids, I'm with my kids. When I'm working, I'm working.

There are always exceptions, but this is the rule.

And, yes, rules are meant to be broken now and then. Let it go.

The One Slow Thing Mantra

It can be easy to give ourselves the impression we need to do every single thing slow and easy all day.

We are always searching for that magic bullet — the fast fix — for what's ailing our lives right now. And, let's face it, some days there is a lot ailing us.

And while we're searching, we realize all that we need to do to change things for the better, and we want to implement them all right now!

Right now.

We think this will finally bring happiness.

I admit I have been guilty of this myself.

The truth is that none of it works when it's all tossed into the same pot at once.

The One Slow Thing per day mantra takes all of that away. We no longer have to do everything slowly — unless it works out that way — and it will if you want it to, eventually.

One Slow Thing per day takes away the guilt and the pressure to be perfect all day long and lets you start with baby steps of slowing down. Maybe you lead up to One Slow Thing per morning and then per afternoon and then per evening. Same for the weekends, too.

Life is so much simpler when we realize we don't need to do everything in one day — not even the slow stuff.

But when we choose do to one slow thing per day, we're permitting ourselves to do something that is possible.

And the possibilities are endless.

The Joy Lives Here Mantra

So many of us are busy doing too much.

And we have many other things we want to do, perhaps that we haven't found the time for in our lives.

Those things are no less important, but there just isn't enough time in the day.

Dinner needs to be made. The floor needs to be swept. The to-dos creep in and pile up and grow like weeds.

Except once you realize that doing the good stuff first makes the other stuff more fun, you learn to trade things around in your schedule. This is when we repeat Joy Lives Here. This is a transition mantra as much as it is a live-in-the-moment mantra.

So set a timer for joy. Actually set a timer on your stove or phone or watch and seek out a fun task for a half hour or longer. Give yourself that gift of play and being in the moment. And once the time runs out, slowly return to your busy life, if you need to.

Setting a timer for joy can work for many things. Set a timer for joy to take care of yourself. Or even for working on a special project that has been on your mind.

This habit of focusing is not about making ourselves slaves to time but rather releasing the hold the to-do list has over us all day long. Eventually, you won't need to set that timer because you will automatically add in the good stuff because it feels good.

The Everything I Need is Here Mantra

We all get in the middle of something and think of something else. We'll talk more about how to avoid this later. But for now it's important to go back to the beginning of this book and think about what you value, what's most important.

If playing and connecting as a family is important, you should know that's all you need right now. I'm not saying all you need to do. I'm saying all you need.

There's a big difference.

What you have to do will get done as it needs to get done and in the order it needs to be accomplished. What you need, however, is a different story and deserves a more prominent place on your to-do list and in your mind.

By saying to yourself repeatedly, "Everything I need is here," you are allowing yourself to relax and feel content, which is the first step to not feeling distracted and torn by all the other things that need to be done.

If you got sick tomorrow, your floors would still be sticky and the grass would need to be mowed, but you wouldn't do any of it because you are sick.

You should take care of your self and your basic needs.

The Stick Together Mantra

Lumping our tasks together is a great time-management technique meant for people in business and careers, but it works wonders at home with a family, too.

When we can lump similar tasks together we save time and, more importantly, energy. An obvious example of this is dusting. You don't usually just dust one room. You'll dust all the rooms at once because that's a natural way to take care of such a task. So when it's time to clean bathrooms, clean them all. When it's time to work outside, take the day to do everything that needs to be done outside.

This stick-together mantra trains your mind to focus on one thing rather than all things.

The Choose the Important Stuff First Mantra

While writing this book, I found myself needing little tiny thinking breaks. So I'd pop on to check email and Facebook for any important notes from readers. Except one second became a half hour. After a few times of catching myself doing this, I started a new mantra: Choose the Important Stuff.

Choose the Important Stuff is a mantra that can be used anytime but particularly when you are doing one thing and should — or could — be doing something else. When you catch yourself wasting time on something you don't want to be doing — sometimes wasting time is perfectly fine when it's the fun stuff you love — then just repeat, "Choose the Important Stuff First."

The It Is What It Is Mantra

This mantra is the most traditional and known of all of these mantras but it's truly a powerful saying to use when you are dwelling on something you cannot control that actually can take up more of your brain power and energy than running or gardening.

When we let things go with a mantra like this we are releasing its hold on us in that moment. This release gives us a chance to move into the next thing on our list or to sink back into the moment we are in right now, the one that is most important.

Distractions of the mind are perhaps the most sneaky time robbers we have in our lives, and yet we rarely address them. We'd much rather address our hours at work or our hours carting kids to their activities. But the truth is I found more time in my life to do the things I love and want to do once I stopped trying to change the world.

Seriously.

I used to be one of those people focused on the world's problems all day long. As a journalist, that's part of the job description. But I still did that long after leaving the newsroom, too.

World issues. Politics. Poverty. News.

It all created busyness in my mind. And while it made me happy to some degree to debate and talk about things that mattered, I also realized after my career in politics that my voice and opinions had little affect on the real change happening.

So I just stopped making those issues a conversation in my head. I still vote and get involved with my hands in areas I can make a real difference, but you will never catch me in a debate in the comments on Facebook about poverty or social issues.

It is what it is. Change what you can change. Let the rest, well, rest.

The Not Right Now Mantra

It's really easy to get caught up in the moment — and that's how distractions happen.

An email that needs a response, for instance, seems easy enough. But when you add a few more emails and a few more responses, the next thing you know you have just taken a half hour to do something that maybe didn't want to do in the first place.

Putting things off is not acceptable for some of us. Some of us value customer service and good communication and feel slighted when someone doesn't get back to us. But think of it this way: Will the difference of responding now rather than two hours from now really matter? We better serve ourselves when we put our needs first and then respond when the time is right.

When we say "Not Right Now" we are metaphorically putting up a wall — a boundary — to protect our time from the world's distractions. About to read a news story ... not right now. About to clean a closet ... not right now. About to take a phone call ... not right now.

There is power in owning your hours. And this mantra helps you get that power back. You deserve to decide how you spend your time. And if you choose emails, then make those intentional.

The Keep it Short Mantra

Sometimes, we get ourselves over-involved in a situation that isn't even our problem.

You can be a savior to people, and if that's your thing, keep doing that. But you can't be a savior to all people, so you have to begin to set boundaries.

Boundaries are the only way to an abundant, more balanced way of living.

But to get there, you have to say things that maybe don't always come out of your mouth. Using phrases such as, "Listen, I'd love to chat with you right now, but I have to keep this short can be helpful.

It seems hard, but it's really that easy.

Keep things short. All of it. Your emails. Your phone calls. Your social media discussions. Save the long, meaningful discussions for when they matter most, which is not every day and which is certainly not all day long.

If you want more time back in your days, you have to be willing to take it back and that might mean speaking up and cutting things short. It may not seem right, but embracing an attitude of non-attachment to other people's needs — aside from your family's, of course — is a very effective way of setting boundaries.

You can still give meaningful advice and get into long conversations — when you want to. But be mindful of those times when you have gone above and beyond what is expected of you in your role.

Life is short.

Emails should be, too.

The Start Where You Are Mantra

Here's the thing: If it were so easy, there wouldn't be millions of books and articles and blog posts telling you how to live more mindfully.

So forget about the guilt and forget about the idea of reaching nirvana and just focus on this moment right here.

As I say all the time, start right where you are right now. And tomorrow do the same thing.

Over time it does get easier, with practice, but it's not ever going to be easy.

Easy is not a word to describe parenting — let alone parenting while trying to be mindful.

Which brings me to this point: I try to avoid the word mindful as often as possible because it's a set up. It's a game we cannot win. You cannot be mindful 24 hours a day, so you shouldn't aspire to doing that.

Aspire to doing just one thing once or twice or three times a day. Aspire to living in the moment at certain moments a day. Aspire to being right here right now and then returning to that state of mind when you can again later.

When we aspire for perfection, we also set up false hopes and unrealistic expectations for those around us. So tell yourself to stop doing expecting more than what people can give — for your sanity and your family's sake.

Savoring Slow Invitation: When you catch yourself doing more than one thing at a time, stop and close your eyes. Grab a cup of steaming hot tea. Gently put an ice cube in your mug of tea. Now watch it until it completely melts and disappears. Your mind is capable of focusing on just one thing. You just proved it. Return to this exercise every time you feel scattered and unable to focus.

Savoring Slow Habit No. 5 | Go Slowly

"There is more to life than increasing its speed." — Mahatma Gandhi

***

What's your hurry, Mama?

Where ya heading so quickly?

Don't you know? This is your life.

This one with the pile of dishes in the sink from last night's dinner.

This one with the piles of clutter that sit around the room, rudely staring at you for attention.

This one with the screaming child with his hands folded across his chest and anger lingering in his heart.

This one with all those Facebook updates of other people's lives, other people's actions, other people's insecurities.

Don't you know your life is happening right now while you're worried about what comes next?

Don't you know your life is happening right now while you're fretting about what just happened?

What are you missing out on?

What beauty is passing you, completely unnoticed?

What memories are you skipping over like a never-ending game of hopscotch?

What's your hurry, Mama?

Where ya heading so quickly?

Don't you know? This is your life.

I wrote the passage above to myself one day when I had that feeling you get when everything feels off and urgent and overwhelming.

Because I live with a sense of urgency every single moment of the day.

I need to always remember that there is no emergency. That we can be late for something and it's OK. That I do not have to always do things by the exact time we've always done them. That it's OK to let things go unfinished.

This chapter is your inspiration to do everything — Every. Single. Thing. — slowly.

Why?

Why move slowly when there is so much to do?

Because it makes everything more meaningful. Think quality over quantity for at least a portion of your day, and you will instantly feel an abundance of time before you.

And sure, it's not always possible to move slowly. But when it is possible try these slow-moment builders.

Of course, before you can start moving more slowly you have to stop yourself from rushing all the time. There will be times to rush. And hurry. Any parent with a child who has trouble making decisions and getting ready for anything on time understands that rushing is just a part of life with kids.

Let that not be the norm, though.

Let the norm include lingering and exploring and wandering and wondering.

Create no-rushing moments through the day. Embrace moments when your child can get lost in their world. These moments can happen anywhere and at anytime. But in order to allow them to happen — in order to make more space and time for them — think about them in advance. Plan out those moments in your day when you know you can just be — and you can just allow your child to be.

Even if you allow it to happen just once in a day, that's better than none at all. And by allowing yourself the gift of just once, you will start to stop, notice and savor slow more often yourself.

Try Parenting Slowly

Anyone who's dealt with a child who takes her sweet time to get dressed and move along in the morning understands the need for rushing.

And yet we know that rushing really robs our feeling of an abundance of time.

Sometimes, it's impossible not to rush. But many other times in our day we can make a conscious effort to just slow everything down that we're doing.

Have you ever been driving along when a car that it is in a huge hurry passes you by — only to have to stop at the next red light? They didn't get further ahead at all. And they missed the scenery being so focused on the next destination.

Same goes for parenting.

If we're not careful, we'll put all of our energy into the next big thing, and we'll forget and miss the little details of this life now.

It all begins with how we flow through our days.

To parent slowly, we must really do everything else slowly, too. Let's begin.

Wake Slowly

One of the more controversial topics I've written and coached mothers on at length is waking early — long before the children to make more time for yourself.

However, there is a real division in our world among those who wake early and those who refuse to wake early.

Regardless of when you wake, the idea of a slow waking routine always feels nice. Often, this is possible only if you've gotten up before the children, though.

To wake slowly means you feel like you can open your eyes when you're ready. But it also means rising and moving along at a slow, enjoyable pace — not in a panic of being late, void of worries and stresses of what needs to be done.

These kinds of mornings are blissful not because they are filled with must-dos but because they are filled with want- to-dos.

Teaching our children to start their mornings this way is such a wonderful life skill. My daughters often join me at the counter with their own binders or journals and sit and write with me. Since TV is off limits all week long, it's never something we have to battle with in the mornings.

Slow mornings can bring a sense of calm to your family's day. They can bring connection in ways you never had before. They can create an atmosphere of sharing fears and worries that may not come up when we're all too busy to think straight.

Creating a beautiful morning routine that helps you feel alive and awake is the difference between jumping out of bed and waking with dread and dragging your feet.

To prepare for a slower morning, set up everything you need for the morning at night (pack lunches, set up breakfast, get clothes ready, for example) and put all of your energy into creating a slow morning intention. Before bed, leave a note for yourself near that first place you go when you wake up as a reminder not to rush or worry today — and just relax. Upon waking, light a candle that signifies a slow, savored morning.

Drink your coffee or tea with two hands on the mug and both eyes staring out at the morning sky. Set up a slow song play list that will lead you through the morning. Classical piano, violin, slow jazz. Anything that inspires you but also feels like it adds space to the air. Anything that brings more depth to your day.

> Savoring Slow Invitation: Create a space in your home for slow morning gatherings. Leave out a meditation cushion if you want to meditate. Clear out a basket for your journal and pens. Gather as a family and read aloud during breakfast. Sticking to the same chapter book all week is not only a great way to have a slow morning but also a great way to sneak in slow learning.

Eat Slowly

Until very recently, I was literally rushing through every meal I ate with my children.

At a restaurant, I would eat slowly and mindfully.

But, at home, I was rushing through meals.

And I was doing it because the behaviors at the table can be so annoying and frustrating I just want to hurry it up and get it over with to move on to the next thing.

Once I realized I was doing this, though, I became aware of all the issues I had around meal time. Dinner should be a beautiful, simple moment to connect and often, really, it was anything but. My expectations were entirely not matching the situation.

So I took a deep breath and created some reminders for myself to eat slowly. To stop between bites to ask a question. To breathe often. To chew thoroughly.

And I taught my children to do the same.

We talked briefly about why it's important to sit up straight and not multitask while eating. And then we learned how to eat mindfully with our eyes closed by eating a piece of dark chocolate.

We still need reminders to eat slowly.

We still rush through our meals on occasion.

We still slow down and relish the food and savor the idea of the hands who made the food.

And you just want it to last a little longer.

So linger longer.

To eat slow, prepare your minds ready with this intention:

Today I want to savor every bite of the food that enters my mouth. May today I take the time not just to chew slowly but to think slowly about the people who made this food possible for our family.

Create slow eating notes to read before and during meals. Frame a meaningful note and put it on the table where you eat. It could be a simple as "Chew Slowly."

Say a prayer or a grace or read a meaningful passage from a book that reminds you to slow down and connect with the feelings you have while being nourished in a healthy way.

Savoring Slow Invitation: Before you touch your fork or your plate, stop for a minute and wait. Close your eyes and take three deep breaths before eating and after just a few bites. Give thanks for the food you are about to eat.

Clean Slowly

Cleaning is not our favorite thing to do.

And it's definitely not our child's favorite thing to do.

What is our favorite, though, is that feeling we get once the house is clean and in order and there's suddenly so much space to create, play and relax.

Clutter really is a downer, and it's normal to start to feel agitated when the house is in chaos.

But rushing through and yelling at everyone to do their part rarely works out well and takes the joy out of your day — and your hours.

So how do you clean slowly?

- **Prepare for slow cleaning.** Slow cleaning doesn't work for a house that is in complete chaos. You will need to declutter first to make this kind of easy, low-pressure cleaning work for your family. De-cluttering before or after dinner is always a great time to get the whole family to put their things away. And then you are ready for the slow cleaning routine all week.

- **Set the mood.** We turn on our Happy Family Playlist as a way to perk ourselves up and get ourselves ready for cleaning together as a family. Nothing gets any of us in the mood more than having some good tunes — and good attitudes.

- **Focus on one or two rooms a day.** This is by far my favorite slow cleaning tip. When I can focus on just the kitchen today, I don't feel scattered and overwhelmed. Choosing one big room and a bathroom or foyer is an easy way to combine rooms so the cleaning can happen Monday through Friday rather than on the weekends.

- **Zen cleaning.** Many of us really enjoy a clean house, and not because we are perfectionists. We like a clean house because if feels like a big cleanse, like all of the bad stuff has gone away and we can start anew. That feeling is found only after the cleaning. To get that feeling while you are cleaning, though, is much harder. Focusing on one task at a time while cleaning is how to avoid that overwhelmed feeling you get while cleaning so many things at once. For each room, write a list of what needs to be done. Pick one of those things and do it. Repeat in each room. This kind of zen cleaning list-making is ideal for children who get overwhelmed as well. This goes back to do one thing — or do nothing.

Listen Slowly

There are always times when you are busy doing something else and a child needs or wants your attention.

And, let's be honest, children need to learn valuable lessons like not interrupting, being patient and how to stand tough in certain situations. But there is nothing better than a really good conversation that is working for both you and your child.

Slow listening allows us to embrace those moments when a

child wants to tell you a long story or ask questions about the world around them.

Slow listening is what builds relationships that are strong and powerful.

This kind of listening doesn't happen when we're distracted. This cannot happen in the middle of making dinner if it's on the stove top.

But it can happen most of the other parts of my day.

And it goes like this.

Stop.

Two eyes.

Two hands.

Stop that other thing you are doing.

Walk over toward the person who needs your attention and give them both of your eyes and look into both of their eyes.

And then make an attempt to put both of your hands on them in a hug or a close connection in some other way.

When we give someone all of our attention, we're fully in that moment. And we're able to fully hear what they are saying so that we can listen to all of the words and feel all of the emotions and concerns that might come out in that conversation.

Savoring Slow Invitation: Challenge yourself to be a slow listener today. When someone is talking to you, stop and look at them and stop doing everything else. See how much you pick up on someone's tone and feelings just by making eye contact and getting down to their level and really listening.

Move Slowly

Aside from those moments when you have to rush, like when you're exercising or rushing out the door to get to work or school, life really should be enjoyed more slowly.

This is not my strength in life. I'm a doer and doers are trying to fit 100 things in a day that really only fits 50.

But, once I intentionally began moving slowly more often, I started to see the benefits. I started seeing how my patience to wait helped my family.

There are many ways to move slowly in a day.

I am not alone when I say that I tend to rush from Point A to Point Z in a day at the speed of light. We have so much we want to "get done" that the only speed we know is Fast and Furious. But we miss so much when we're in that high gear with blinders over our eyes. We miss the way the trees are still and full of birds. We miss the way an elderly man waves at the kids. We miss making eye contact with the store greeter. Going through life as an explorer is a wonderful way to slow down.

Explore Slowly

Wander and roam. You will wonder and seek. You will not only ask questions but try and find the answers. You will daydream long enough for everything in your mind to come full circle.

What will we find around the bend? What's down that path? What's up that tree? How does this bark feel? What would the cool creek water feel like on our feet? What does that puppy's fur feel like?

Stop to pet the dogs.

Stop to smell the roses.

Stop to read a sign.

Stop to rest.

Stop to talk.

This is how we explore the world around us more slowly. More awake.

Exploring slowly is one of my favorite things to do. It's really about letting go and releasing all control. Here are some ideas for including slow exploring into your week:

- **Take a Slow Walk:** These kinds of walks are meant to be enjoyed. Stopping to see the worms on the sidewalk. Stopping to smell flowers. Stopping to talk to neighbors. Stopping to listen to the pond full of bull frogs.

- **Let the Kids Lead:** Letting children or teenagers take over the lead of where you will go is the best way to go on a slow exploration. This kind of child-led exploring can only lead to discovering new wonders and miracles, such as stumbling upon wild horses or hot air balloons.

- **Think Like a Child:** Children are amazed at everything they see. They question everything they see. They wonder about everything — and everyone — they see. This is how you can slow time.

Enjoy Weekends Slowly

For many of us, the weekends are the time to catch up for what didn't get done all week.

But, really, we know that's not the way a weekend should go. And so by Sunday night, we're exhausted and often feeling like we didn't get a chance to rest, recharge and get that meaningful family time we do deserve.

And there are weekends when that's just going to be the case.

What my family loves to do now, though, is plan as best as we can to avoid that weekend rush. How?

By doing the hard work all week so the weekends are left for just play.

Getaway at Home

There have been years when a vacation for our family was impossible. And yet those years, it seemed, were the ones when we needed it most. I coped with new ways to enjoy each week — turning regular weekends into more meaningful, relaxing days. I am hopeful that this list of ideas will spark and inspire your creativity to live your summer weekends — and any weekend all year long — to the fullest.

7 Ways to Vacation at Home

- **Staycation:** From lazy mornings and easy breakfasts to having a backyard picnic, the best part of vacation is doing very little. I mean so little it is almost boring — almost.

- **Re-discover the simple things:** Drink sweet iced tea and eat cookies for an afternoon snack. Add wine to your dinners. Fluff up your pillows. (A friend of mine even bought all white bedding once for their staycation so it would feel more like a hotel experience.) Freeze things like scones, granola and pancakes so that you can just heat up and enjoy.

- **Read:** Read a travel book. Travel to places you've never been on the Internet. Read about faraway places in travel literature. Dream a lot. Maybe even devour a beach read while lounging outside on a blanket.

- **Head to the water:** Even a day on the local lake or a creek is relaxing. Plan to indulge a bit with your feet in some water. Water is eye candy for the soul. At the very least, a long hot bath will do.

- **Do little cooking:** I cook nearly every meal we eat — from scratch. It's crazy, but I love it. But even I admit that it can burn a person out and that a week spared of throwing together big, fresh meals is dreamy. Instead turn fresh fruit, veggies, cheese and bread into a meal.

- **Only clean the serious messes:** Assuming the house is clean when you start — and that you have to clean it when it's over — a weekend is not too long to just let it all go. Really, it isn't.

- **Watch the stars and the sky:** Once the kids are asleep, sneak outside for just a few minutes to sit and soak in the wonder of the stars and the big sky. This is one of those subtle, meaningful moments that can turn an average day into amazing. Relish in the great wonders of the Earth.

Play Slowly

There are only 24 hours in a day and between work and school and sleep, we are lucky if we have a good hour to play together.

So make a point to go out of your way for that hour — or a half hour — and just play slowly.

Slow play means not rushed. Not hurried. Not bossy do-it-my-way play. It means let your kid do your hair or teach you that game you have no idea what the rules are or toss the ball back and forth a million times because that's what she wants to do right now. It means playing school for a half hour where you pretend you don't know how to add or spell anything, and he has to teach you.

The point is not the time.

The point is not the want.

The point is a set period of time in your mind, body and soul to being there in full, undivided attention.

Just being there with no adult agenda.

Savoring Slow Invitation: Practice give and take. Attempt to offer a half hour session of play in return for a half hour of something else that you need to do, like making dinner or doing homework together. This give and take is a great way to be productive and still play together.

Work Slowly Together

Sometimes it feels like there's no good time for homework. Kids need a break as soon as they get home. They are too busy before dinner. And after dinner they start to lose focus and get too tired.

And you have a lot to do as well.

Creating a slow homework zone, however, is a lovely way to energize the dreaded hour while also still getting things done.

Grab your own "work," whether it be next week's menu planning or a cleaning list or a work project, and turn on some tunes and grab some snacks — if the timing works — and work together, slowly. No hurry because this is the fun. Help out as needed but mostly do your own thing that needs to be done.

Slow reading and storytelling

There are stories.

And there are stories that come alive.

There are books.

And there are books that come alive.

Reading and telling stories slowly, without a rush or a hurry, are the most magical moments in a child's life. Stories contain powerful lessons but not as much if we rush through the lessons, the conflict, the mystery, the suspense.

Here are some storytelling tips that can help your stories come alive:

- Use loud and soft voices.
- Get up and move around, acting out the story.
- Ask a lot of questions.
- Give yourself ample time to tell a story.
- Involve your child as much as possible.
- Bring out some fun props to help bring life to the story.

Bedtime is not meant to be rushed. It's meant to be cherished because when our children are teenagers and beyond we won't be doing this ritual every night.

So enjoy it now while it lasts.

Savoring Slow Invitation: Tell your children a story about a time from your own childhood that embodies the savoring slow experience. Use this story as a way to both tell an interesting story but also to demonstrate that slow can be fun and exciting.

Savoring Slow Habit No. 6 | Do Less

—————

"It is not enough to be busy. So are the ants. The question is: What are we busy about? — Henry David Thoreau

***

I've tried a million ways to figure out how to stop being so busy, and I've found only one real way to do that: do less.

But we can't do less, can we?

Things won't get done.

Our lives will fall apart.

Right?

Perhaps all of it is not quite as serious as we make it out to be. Perhaps — as we discussed during Savoring Slow Habit "Release" — our world really won't fall apart.

In fact, when we can actually figure out ways to do less — especially of the stuff we dislike — we can create an an amazing amount of energy in our lives. We have more motivation for other

—————

things rather than feeling weighed down by all the burdens we have on our shoulders.

This habit is the best one if you can be strong enough to do it.

It's not easy to do less in a society where we're always pushed to do more, give more, and buy more.

Which is why this is a good habit to start.

Doing less doesn't mean lazy, even though sometimes it might feel that way.

Doing less doesn't mean doing nothing, even though that might be nice sometimes.

Doing less doesn't mean giving up on life, even though you probably feel that way right now before you even start this habit.

Doing less will actually make you more productive.

Doing less will add energy back into your days — not to mention many other positive emotions, too.

Doing less is a way of life, a practice and it begins right here, where you are right now.

This chapter will lead you on a journey to doing less — not nothing, just less.

We begin where you least expect.

In your bank account.

Spend less

The first month we tried to spend nothing, we didn't feel much of a change.

But by the second month, our lives started to see a dramatic slowing down effect.

Weekends became more relaxing. We were actually more productive.

When we cut out everything associated with spending money, our many options just melt away, naturally simplifying our days and nights — and our home.

Life becomes more streamlined and more spacious for things like reading and exploring — and good long naps or laying in the grass gazing at the clouds.

Give yourself a tiny budget to use as fun money. When it's gone, it's gone.

Not always easy, I realize, but it's one of the best places to start, especially when you are feeling overwhelmed by life.

Stop spending money on just about everything.

Stop spending money on entertainment.

Stop spending money on things.

Stop spending money on activities and events.

All of that time spent spending adds up. Less time in busy stores means more time doing what you love.

All of that extra money in your bank account adds up. More money in the account means saving for more meaningful things like better vacations and, perhaps, hiring a lawn service to take care of the grass that you plan to lay in and gaze at the clouds.

Savoring Slow Invitation: Enjoy a spend-free day or a spend-free month. Work it into the calendar so there is food in the fridge and birthday presents are bought. But the rest — the other stuff — can just wait. If you try this and it doesn't work the first time, try it again. Habits are hard to break.

Own less

Don't you just love clutter?

I didn't think so.

Very few modern mothers today will say they love clutter, or cleaning up or putting things away.

And yet the stuff keeps piling up.

The natural next step to spending less is owning less.

Of course, we live in a materialistic world. Everything is replaceable and easy to acquire. Our homes are barely big enough to hold all of this stuff.

But when we make an intentional choice to spend less, we actually make a conscious effort to own less.

Less stuff means less to pick up, clean, put away, find a place for, organize, give away and throw away.

And all of that energy spent dealing with stuff is freed up, creating a significant release on the hold our possessions have over our time.

We start to see the value in simplicity. The beautiful basics of just being here on this earth. Stuff no longer attracts us like the birds do when they are gathering nesting materials in the front yard. Suddenly, there is time to tackle those weeds in the flower garden and, while we're there, pick a few flowers to put in a vase.

Stuff shouldn't own us anymore than our chores and our errands and our jobs do.

When we start to evaluate the power our stuff has on us, we start to see patterns in why our rooms look the way they do. Of course, we can always keep buying more storage bins and storage shelves, but the truth is that we just need to curb the number of things we are bringing into our lives.

But the kids? They want so many things!

I get that. I do.

There are many ways to teach children how to want less things, but my favorite way is simply to talk to them about how we could better spend our money. Rather than buy a toy they will outgrow, we could spend it on a weekend away or a piece of furniture that will last many years.

Usually children are able to come around over time. But if they still really want that humongous dolphin stuffed animal and they saved their money for it, then so be it. They have to learn the value of things before they can learn the lesson.

Here are a few questions to ask yourself before you buy anything. Anything at all.

- Will I use this next week or next month or next year?

- Do I have a place for this in my home?

- Is it beautiful and will it make our home — or us — feel happier?

- Why do I really want this right now?

If you've answered all of these questions and you still want to buy your item of choice, at least you know you've made an intentional purchase.

Savoring Slow Invitation: Think about all the stuff you have right now sitting in boxes and closets. You are overwhelmed, right? You can't decide whether to keep it or get rid of it. The sentimental gifts of things you would never display in a million years might be worth keeping. But if there is no value — no connection to you

— let it go. Make a list of all the things you think you might want to part ways with and start listing the connection you have to that item. Decide what to keep and what to get rid of based on that list.

Do less

With the absence of all that time being spent out in restaurants and museums and other special events and activities, and with the absence of less buying and spending and less stuff to clean and organize and donate, what is left?

Less to do. Fewer places to be. Less to clean. Less to stress over, argue over and fret about.

If you spend a little less, you will have more time. If you spend a lot less, you will have a lot more time.

We learned the value of less on our summer vacation at the beach a year ago.

The four of us stayed comfortably in a tiny, 500-square-foot condo that overlooks the ocean. With one bedroom, one tiny bathroom and a kitchenette with only a stove, not an oven, the living quarters should have seemed small and abnormally confining for us since we're used to our modest, suburban home with three bathrooms and a large yard.

And other than sharing that single bathroom, I must say that everything was just ... easier.

So little stuff. So much less to clean. Less to fuss over. Less to cook. Less to eat, in general. Fewer options. Fewer art supplies.

We had one option for each meal. We had one game. We had three movies. We had two books each. I had one legal pad to write in — and it was filled with amazing new ideas for my business and blog.

And we were happy — happy because all that mattered were two things: We were together as a family without any distractions, and we could wake up and see the ocean every morning.

The secret to happiness is simple.

It's true that when we choose the simple path, we really choose a more peaceful way of living. This is the key to happiness. The secret of living a full life versus planning a life.

After we were home from the beach, I wanted desperately to cling to the simple life we had all week, but I could already see it slipping away. The grass needed to be mowed, and the weeds were taller than my children and the van needed to be de-sanded.

The children went back to bickering over small things. The dining room table became cluttered with too many art supplies.

Suddenly, it became very clear that all of our luxuries and extra amenities felt like more work that would take us away from matters — more time together.

When we say slow down, what do we really mean?

Do we mean doing less stuff?

Do we mean going slower?

Do we mean going back in time to the old days, simpler times?

The first obstacle to wanting to slow down and not being able to make it happen is not about changing what's on your calendar so much as it is about knowing.

It's about knowing what you are looking for.

Savoring Slow Invitation: This week, assess your family's to-dos. List all the things you need to do, want to do, have to do. Make the list as long as it needs to be. In other words, put it all on there. On the same list, write down all the things you are worried about — things that take time away from your mental energy. Write them all down as well. Write down next to each of those items how much money they cost your family each month. At the end, circle only the things you absolutely have to do — as in it's a matter of life or death — and the things that make your hearts really, really happy. What's left on the list?

Going back in time to simpler days

It's so easy to go to the store to buy laundry detergent.
One-two and done.
So why do I keep making our own every year?
Because it feels slower. It feels fresher. It feels simpler.
It takes about a half hour to get the ingredients and mix them together.
But that is pure love in that labor of grinding that soap.
And things bloom and blossom where we put our love.
I'm a big fan of the Do-it-Yourself movement, but not for everything.
Some things are just done better at the store.
Perhaps it's my age, but I'm starting to see more value in the simpler things we can do around our busy, chaotic homes to bring a bit of peace and whimsy.

These activities are not necessarily doing less. But they feel more meaningful because they are using our brains in different ways. What was an ordinary routine task comes alive once we do it differently. We enjoy doing everyday tasks more when they seem new and interesting. This gives us the appearance of doing less even if it's not less at all. Anytime we use our hands to make something or do something differently we are waking up our senses, which makes us feel alive and awake.

I encourage you to try doing things differently, too. Hang your laundry outside. Bake your own bread. Unplug the TVs and video games and play a board game. Make jam. Use the stove to cook popcorn. Make s'mores the real way, outside with a fire, if you can. Play hide and seek. Drive a different way, maybe even the slower route.

Modern technology is great — and 90 percent of the week, it saves us so much time and hassle. But for 10 percent of your week (or more), pretend like it doesn't exist. Light candles and do things the old-fashioned way for a change of pace.

And you will instantly begin Savoring Slow — as well as gain a new appreciation for modern amenities.

Putting boundaries on the chores

Ask any child what they dislike the most at home, and they will likely say chores.

I was the same way.

What I try to relay to my kids is that I don't enjoy them either, but that we can have more fun as a family if we can all get them done quickly and effortlessly.

And so we work hard in many ways to do just that.

But to be honest, it would be great to just not have to do chores one day.

Chores aren't much fun unless we make them fun. So make them fun. Turn them into something wild and beautiful.

And when you are caught up — and you never will be — stop for a day and let them all pile up again.

And just celebrate as a family with a chore-free Saturday.

Yes, a Chore-Free Day.

I said it.

Why not? Who's going to police the fact that you didn't clean the bathroom for one week? Are the children going to be forever ruined because you didn't make them clean?

This goes right along with my Yes Mama attitude. Why a whole day without chores?

You deserve it. You need it. You will be better for it.

Reconstruct the family meal

I'd like to take issue with the family meal.

And how boring it can feel.

And how routine it has become.

And how if you aren't making a big meat-and-potatoes dinner and putting it on the table at 5 o'clock when everyone can gather around, then you are failing your family.

Modern mothers don't have time for that kind of dinner. Not even on a Sunday half the time.

So let's reconstruct the family meal. Let's give ourselves permission to make it up.

What is a family meal?

It's when we are all together — or mostly all together — and we're eating a meal.

That's it.

There's no set definition that says it needs to be a two-course meal or sitting around a table.

Family meals at our house have happened in the back of our mini-van when it was too cold to picnic outdoors. Family meals at our house have happened on the front porch on a really great night.

And what's on the plates for those meals?

Whatever we can put together that allows for the most family time.

Leftovers.

Cheese and crackers.

In all honestly, children want our time, not some big fancy dinner. They'd much rather choose a quick and easy meal and get back to playing together.

And, really, theres's nothing wrong with that.

> Savoring Slow Invitation: Give yourself permission to change the way you've viewed dinner in the past. If you aren't cooking, you can easily throw together a healthy meal of snacks that aren't fast food. Pile them in a picnic basket and eat them wherever you are — together.

Beyond the chores and activities

I have had slow days with my daughters that felt like they lasted a week.

Depending on their moods and needs, I could easily find myself exhausted and tapped out of ideas by 10 a.m.

We want to raise happy, thriving children, so we tend to overdo everything for them as a result.

Figuring out how to balance our yeses and nos all day long can be a battle for a busy family. But understanding that children need to feel empowered is absolute liberation for parents.

Teaching children to do for themselves what you have been doing for them for a long time is the best time saver in the world. But it also takes time and patience. They may seem physically capable, but they may not be emotionally or developmentally ready.

Beyond the everyday matters, though, our children need to know that we rely on them to do their part around the house. We call it helping the family.

We do not bark orders and tell them to do their chores or else. We explain to them that we need their help. We simply can't do it all on our own.

Before you go off delegating, though, make sure you understand the purpose here is not to teach children a lesson or to create less work for you.

It's to create more family time in general. When everyone works together, more time and space is created.

And that is the beauty of everyone working together to get things done.

This, of course, includes partners. Getting them on board is just as important as children. It doesn't take much effort to sweep a floor now and then or grab toys off the floor. For the littlest children the effort doesn't even need to be on chores as much as it should be on teaching them to take care of themselves —

get themselves dressed, brush their hair and teeth and, even, help with their breakfast by putting jelly on toast.

Every little bit from every single person really makes a world of difference in the home — and to your busy day.

Savoring Slow Invitation: Create a family household chores calendar and list. Spread everything out so it's done over time, making sure to leave time and space for chore-free days, spend-free months and other special days. Invite your family to a Slow Table Talk to discuss. Explain that your time simply doesn't allow for all of this to get done, and you need help from everyone. Set a timeline for when things will get done and how you will celebrate as a family when the house is, finally, clean.

Savoring Slow Habit No. 7 | Plug-In

"The art of concentration is a continual letting go. We let go of what is inessential or distracting. We let go of a thought or a feeling, not because we are afraid of it or because we can't bear to acknowledge it as a part of our experience; but, because it is unnecessary." — Sharon Salzberg, "Unplug: For an Hour, a Day, or a Weekend"

***

One of the best things I've done for myself in the past couple years is cut my dependency on email and social media as a way to start my day.

To challenge myself to do something else in the mornings as I rise and wake up gave me a look at what life can be like without staring at a screen.

That led to more unplugging all day.

I now only plug in to do work and write, and the rest of the time I'm busy doing other things — including doing writing away from the computer by hand.

As many reasons as there are to unplug, though, there are just as many reasons to plug in.

It seems everything we need is online now, and yet nothing we need is online.

It's a constant battle to keep up and put down.

Don't unplug indefinitely. Be intentional about when you plug in.

What's the difference?

There's a difference between living life unplugged all the time and plugging in at intentional times throughout your day, when it matters most and when you need it most.

Just because you love your online connections, doesn't mean the Internet has to own you. Modern parents now use blogs and social media more than parenting books so these connections are important.

The trick is understanding how to balance it. Choosing to plug-in when the time is right let's you regain control that technology has taken from you.

This shift in how you use technology can be really beautiful. Instead of spending all day on the computer, make a concerted effort to be unplugged all day and plug in at the right times and under certain conditions.

This habit is not an easy one to begin and implement, but it is the quickest way to feel less tired and burned out. And once you become less dependent on random social media for your own energy and motivation, you find more time for doing the things that bring authentic motivation to your family.

Such as hikes in the woods where no cell phone tower will reach.

Or building a tree house with your own two hands.

Savoring Slow Invitation: Think about what you need to be online for during your non-working hours. Write a list of all those online must-dos and put them first on your list for when you do plug in. Once you've done that, you can start to prioritize what needs your time online. Save the generic, numbing out, scanning social media for a set time or two during the day and leave it at that.

Plug-in to your Savoring Slow Adventures List

Neurologists have been studying our perception of time for decades.

And one thing is very clear.

We perceive new experiences in deeper, more meaningful ways than any other experiences.

This explains why when you go beyond your comfort zone, you remember that moment so much more than, say, your same-old, same-old drive to work this morning.

With children, almost everything is a new experience, which might explain why they constantly live in the present moment and feel like the world is their oyster.

We can get that same feeling when we choose to live life to the max.

Rather than focusing on unplugging to gain more time, focus on doing something new. If unplugging seems scary, consider baby steps first and then work your way up to longer periods of time. For 15 minutes. For 30 minutes. For one hour.

Focus on creating Savoring Slow adventures instead.

If you want to do things. Accomplish things. Write things. Make things. Entertain. Socialize. Travel. Stare at the clouds. Read more. Well, then, it's really hard to do all of that when you are watching TV or scanning Facebook for the latest friend update.

And the sooner you explain that to your children, the better.

If all they know is TV or video games, they aren't going to have the creativity or imagination to think of anything else to do.

Your adventure lists can vary from anything you want to do at home or in your home to anything you want to explore outside your home. It can have big ideas. And it can — and should — contain small ideas.

Living still happens in the details, in the margins of our lives. While waiting for a child to get ready for school. While waiting for dinner to finish cooking. While waiting for a bath to run. All of these moments, when you might pick up your phone, are also opportunities.

You could create monthly or seasonal bucket lists to make sure you don't miss out on a thing that has to do with this particular time of year. We'll talk more about this later in the book, though.

Not every bullet on your list needs to be extravagant or life changing. They can be simple and meaningful. And by keeping the list going, you are sure to add to it.

So the next time a child is grabbing for their device, suggest they grab for their bucket list instead. For a younger child, ask them what they want to do today. For an older child, ask them, "Did you ever land that handstand?" "How's that book coming along you wanted to read?"

And then ask them to show you.

Or wait and watch them while they practice and learn and try and perfect their own goal.

Waiting embodies the Savoring Slow spirit completely.

Savoring Slow Invitation: Try going for a walk without your phone. And then a drive. And then a whole day. And see how it feels. Keep a journal of your unplugged adventures. See how much fun you can have without being plugged in and log it as a family.

Establish tech-free zones

When I first started blogging, I went to bed with my cell phone next to me. I'd check it several times before going to sleep. I'd check it first thing in the morning while still groggy and seeing blurry.

And then I graduated to an iPad, which was so liberating and so I found myself doing more work than usual while in bed and right after waking.

Then it hit me.

I was literally sleeping with my devices.

Ever since that day, I have never kept my devices next to my bed. I simply plug them both in across the room and my bed, my sanctuary, is free of the noise of the Internet and my work demands.

Over time, my husband has slowly changed his ways as well. He no longer plugs in right next to the bed and I haven't seen him reading sports updates late at night when he can't sleep.

Our family mission includes being more intentional and awake to the life we are living. So we have decided to try and limit the use of social media while together.

It's your life, and you get to decide how distracted and filled up you want your days to be.

But if you want less virtual world and more real connections, you will have to start by setting boundaries.

Creating a tech-free zone is one way to Savor Slow in the times of your day when you are most likely free and able to enjoy life, but more inclined to pick up your phone and just zone out on social media or reading email.

By creating this boundary, I also cured that sense of urgency I had for the longest time on checking email. I still check email plenty during the day, but I have made a point not to do so first thing in the morning or last thing before bed. This is how I set up my own boundaries to reduce the hold email had over my life. Now it's easy for me to wait a half a day to respond to an email.

Many women are not sure how to get their husbands on board for such an idea, though.

Start by announcing to your family that you are creating spaces in the home that should be phone and device free. Ask for their ideas, but you can suggest the kitchen, for instance, or a family room where you gather the most for conversation and connecting. Or the bedrooms, since they are a place to recharge and reconnect as well.

Explain why this is important to you and be patient as they explore what that means over time. As the devices creep back in

— and they will — use gentle reminders of how great it felt to be in each others' company with less distractions and clutter.

Additionally, be prepared to do things together that are device-free, so that those rooms don't just become a ghost town while everyone retreats elsewhere. The idea is to create more real-life connections, not less.

Tech-Free Zones can expand beyond declaring rooms, too. It could mean no devices on family vacation or on Sundays. It could even be as simple as taking a walk without any phones — or cameras.

- Go on a hike.

- Try out a sport or a new exercise.

- Form a family book club (or comic book club.)

- Redecorate a room with everyone's input.

- Cook a meal or bake together (let the kids decide.)

- Take a road trip to a neighboring town.

- Visit a lake or creek and go wading.

- Camp in the backyard.

Experiment with a family tech hour

Our guilt-o-meter definitely rises when our kids seem to ask for nothing but TV time.

But learning to plug-in at the right time is another lesson for your children.

Once you all start living more unplugged all the time, rather than plugging in so much that you need to unplug, you can start to find the right times to get back online.

At our house, we've been playing with the idea of a Family Tech Hour on the weekends and days off from school as a way to set boundaries on our amount of plugged-in time.

A family tech hour is a simple concept, like most things in this book. It's not a stressor. It's not mandatory. And it's not aimed to put anyone down for what they like or don't like.

It's simply a way to say yes to technology — for everyone.

We all have our vices online. It might be a game. A video. A website. Or searching for new ideas to make life more interesting.

As a family who intentionally chooses to plug in, you can simply dedicate one hour — maybe two — when everyone is given complete permission to simply plug-in and zone out.

For that time frame, everyone gets to choose how they want to spend that time. We all play or watch videos or get our work done (like paying the bills or doing some emails), and then we're done.

Time's up. Move on. Get outside. Get fresh air. Do something creative. Be active in YOUR life. Get back to that bucket list.

And all is good in the world.

Savoring Slow Invitation: Experiment with a one-hour tech hour this weekend. Give yourselves a chance to let technology in without bargaining power, without negotiations and without arguments. Just let it happen. And you indulge, too, because this hour is not just for the kids. It's for the whole family. The trick, though, is making sure you are only plugging in for that hour and not sneaking it in the rest of the day — or else it is not effective.

Plug-in to nature

As we drove into the parking area of the park for a hike, we wondered if we were even at a park. It looked more like a piece of land that had been forgotten about.

First, set back miles from main roads, then down a long gravel path, and beyond that a tiny, rustic patch of gravel where cars could park, if any were around.

But there weren't many. Just one. And no one nearby.

"I'm going to just stay in the car, Mama," my daughter said.

"We can do this," I told her. "It's an adventure. We're brave."

I looked at the signal on my cellphone.

There wasn't one.

We can do this, I told myself.

We trudged up the hill. Rocks, large and small, covered the path, our feet struggled to find solid ground. It had just rained. The mud between the rocks was slick. We had to be careful not to slip.

At the top of the steep hill, they learned how to pee in the woods without getting their bottoms wet. They learned how to follow trail blazes. They learned how to cross barren creeks, pass broken roots that looked like caves.

My daughter pointed out everything — leaves, rocks, bark — shaped like hearts because she knows I love to find surprise hearts.

Once we'd been hiking up the hill long enough for our bodies to be sweaty and we started wondering if we were doing this right, we met another hiker and her son.

"You are about half way there," she said. "It's a lot farther than you think."

At the top, finally, victory.

We survived a desolate hike in a remote landscape of woods and mountains with only water bottles and each other.

This made me think we can survive more days without a cellphone connection.

Savoring Slow Invitation: Challenge yourself to start thinking about your need to carry your cellphone. Sure, when you are away from the kids and the sitter or the school might call, fine. But when you are all together, who else is going to call or need you for a few hours? How urgent will that call be? Just how long could you go without a cell phone attached to your body?

Plug-in to get stuff done

Lists keep me on task, and I can't get by without at least one or two a day.

I love lists and how they ensure I am doing what needs to be done while also slipping in and out of the routine to spend time as a family or doing something kind for myself.

I value a really good list.

And one of my favorite lists is my time online list.

This is as simple as it sounds. I write a list of what I have to do online, and I set a timer to make sure I stick to those things and only those things.

It's best to estimate the time needed for each task and determine how much time over all you need online. If you have to pay bills and check email, you can estimate that as about a half hour. Do you need to be online more than that to do other things? OK, then estimate one hour and set your timer for that time.

If there is time left over, guess what? You can check in on that friend you haven't heard from in a year on Facebook or search for new recipes on Pinterest.

Or later you can just add a social media block of time to your list. Social time is important and should absolutely be factored into your life. Many of us have valuable connections online, and we need to keep those friendships going because they make us feel good. So just factor that time in as your plug-in time and then let it go.

You will never be able to catch everything, and that's when releasing comes back around, once again.

By creating an online to-do list, you will minimize the time you spend searching around aimlessly. Your list is your guide.

You are your tour guide, and only you know the way home.

Savoring Slow Invitation: Take a moment before hopping online to write a detailed list of everything you need — and want —

to do online this week. Using a weeklong list will allow you to take less time online at a time while also doing just one thing at a time. Be sure to write down your must-read blogs. Write down paying bills. Write down scanning Facebook for important friend updates. And make sure to estimate how much time you will need and try to stick to that time.

Plug-in to the values and benefits of technology

There are a lot of studies that tell us that computer use is bad. That screens are bad. That it's all bad, bad, bad.

But the truth is that it's not all bad. And the more we say no to our children about computers or cellphones, the more they want them.

And so I want to leave you with this message.

There are really good things about technology and the games our children play. There is value in it all.

With moderation and balance.

Screen use should never be chosen over doing real-life building and games, but it is definitely a source of fun and joy for many.

Teach your children how to balance it, too, by showing them there is more to life than a screen. But give them the time they need to learn and explore it, too.

While none of us wants a child who is constantly playing games or watching TV, we also could stand to take a chill pill in this area of technology, too. A little isn't too much, and, once we realize that, the resistance will fade away — and maybe so will the requests.

Savoring Slow Invitation: Accept that sometimes screens are an appropriate way for a child, especially one who might be tired, to recharge and reconnect with themselves. Say yes to trusting that they know what they need sometimes. And forgive yourself from any guilt for those days when they do seem to want to do nothing but watch TV.

Savoring Slow Habit No. 8 |Unstructured

"Live slow enough and there is only the beginning of time. Follow anything in its act of being, a snowflake falling, ice melting, a loved one waking and we are ushered into the ongoing moment of the beginning. The quiet instant from when each breath starts. What makes this moment so crucial is that it continually releases the freshness of living. The key to finding this moment and all its freshness again and again is in slowing down." — Mark Nepo, in "The Book of Awakening."

***

These days, every single place you go someone is telling you about being a mindful parent.

And you really want to be that kind of parent who doesn't tell their kids "just a minute" or "maybe later."

But you also have a house to keep clean and organized. And probably a job or a project that needs to be done. And you probably also have other things lingering, like bills to pay, meals to plan, grocery lists to make.

Because all of these things we do to keep a smooth-running

home contribute greatly to a peaceful home life, and you know this, so you want to keep the peace flowing.

Except it's always a juggle. Choosing this over that. Now over later. Cleaning over playing.

I've been a present and mindful parent for my girls' entire lives. There when they wake up, there when they go to sleep and there in all those moments in between — with some exceptions.

But I still have taken many moments away to do my own thing, to tend to other matters and to focus on other things. We simply cannot be entertaining them and be entertained by them all day long every single day, forever.

Research says that we are with our kids more now than ever. We're more engaged, more connected and more active in their lives than ever.

I believe it.

I've lost track of the hours I've spent watching my girls play, grow up, talk, fight, eat, draw, dance ...

And these are memories I will never forget.

But for the sake of time management and sanity — as well as our children's best interests — we have to be conscious about how we're over-parenting because we think it's the mindful thing to do.

I like to say that I am the love child between the helicopter parents and the free-range parents.

The best parents give love freely but they also let their children explore freely, too.

I want to be active and engaged with my daughters' lives while still offering a lot of space and unsupervised play for them to grow and solve their own problems in life.

I want them to know that I am here for questions but not be put in the middle of the drama. I am here to role play but not to play every single minute of the day.

A healthy balance can — and should — be the goal.

What does this have to do with busy?

Over-parenting can lead to over-busy. Over-parenting leads to burned-out parents. Over-parenting means bitter and sour parents.

There is engaged and active and loving. And there is smothering and obsessed.

This book is for those in the middle, the ones who want to let go and be hands-on.

What? You're thinking this isn't possible.

It absolutely is very much possible. My husband and I are living examples.

When the kids need us, we are there. When they need space, they get it.

If you aren't busy over-parenting, you have more time for yourself, for your marriage, for your home.

More time to think and clean, if you will.

But how do we release this control when we're all supposed to be mindful 24/7?

I'm as mindful as you can get with my daughters, but even I'm not willing to give undivided attention to my children's every single request and desire. If I did, the house would be in total chaos and nothing would get done, not even the dishes.

My younger twin, alone, gets about 9.5 invisible boo-boos a day. I simply can't stop and cater to every single scratch and paper cut. I'd never have time for anything.

When did we get here? Where we have to be "on" all the time?

But here's the bigger reason why we must release ourselves

from being mindful all day long: We're not any good as parents that way because we're tired and overwhelmed. We've lost our energy by 10 a.m. We are zonked out by 8 p.m. There's suddenly no living in our life.

What this comes down to is knowing your own boundaries and also empowering our children to be more independent and less reliant on our praise and accolades.

Does this mean neglecting our children?

Of course not. This is about spending quality time with our children and not quantity. They remember when we're half-there, half-listening and half-paying attention.

Empowering our kids to be fearless, brave and curious without restrictions is how to make them feel ready to take on the world — without needing our hand or our gentle nudges. And it's about empowering ourselves to be confident as engaged, active parents who give their children plenty of space to roam and learn.

The beauty is always in the middle.

And it's a journey, not a destination. Just like being mindful isn't easy to do, practicing the art of wandering isn't either.

When we can surrender to an unstructured day, we surrender to this wonderful world we're a part of that includes our children. There is so much to take in. I often wonder just how much I miss when I stick to such a strict routine and schedule.

Like the day I saw an opossum in the yard across the street while sitting on our front porch.

We're often so busy doing the exact same thing at the exact same time — with good reason, because kids love consistency — that we do forget to stop and look around and just breathe while standing still and with no agenda.

Unstructured routines

My family thrives on routines.

We like consistency and patterns to our days — even our weekends.

But we don't like to feel tied down.

There is a fine balance to having structure and routine while still allowing for a lot of flow in our days for spontaneity and learning.

The amazing benefit to creating flexible and unstructured family routines is that they leave space in your day for problems to be solved, for conversations to take place, for teachable moments to unfold.

There are simple ways to add unstructured time into your everyday moments.

There will be times when you have to put your foot down and keep a routine, such as when homework or a project have to be done. But there are many other times when you can relax and lighten up on what gets done when, such as at bedtime when a child wants to color before bed instead of reading.

Maybe the coloring is exactly what he needs right now. We only learn these things by allowing this kind of flexibility in our days.

Savoring Slow Invitation: For one day, play around with your own concept of routine. Let the bedtime go a little later. Allow for a little more fun in the mornings before breakfast. Let go of your idea of what things are supposed to be like and just enjoy the time you have together.

Unstructured learning

Many of the moms I work with have said they feel the most guilt over not doing activities with their kids. They feel like they should be doing art and learning activities found online all day long.

What all of those great idea posts forget to factor in is that you're busy doing everything else all day, and there's often not enough hours — or money — to do it all.

That is your reality. Busy and overwhelmed and wanting to be more present, peaceful and playful.

And so the best thing to remember is that unstructured play is actually really good for your children. It gives them the grit they need to be successful adults.

Whatever activities you choose only enhance their life. Give yourself permission to create more space in your day for unstructured learning — those moments when you take extra time to watch children trying to tie their shoes or reach something on a higher shelf. Watch how they problem solve and figure things out and be there to help if you are needed.

Savoring Slow Invitation: Doodle your routine for the day as it naturally flows from one thing to the other — without any strict time barriers or serious adult agendas. Just draw little pictures of what happens and what you do. And then let the day go.

Unstructured play time

I'll admit that when my daughters were younger — and even now — I have intervened way too much into their sibling arguments.

I just want them to be happy and get along!

It took many years for me to realize that my intervention in their heated arguments wasn't really serving them well, that they needed to learn to get along on their own without my presence.

This kind of unstructured playtime is valuable. We need to learn to let them work it out, and when we do, we offer them unstructured playtime as well.

Of course, there are children who don't want to play on their own. They need confidence and ideas. And that's OK, too.

You sometimes have to teach them how to be independent and imaginative.

And for the really worried child who needs you to be there for every single thing, here are a few tips you can use to encourage them to take risks and build their confidence:

- **Start an Adventure Journal.** We started a family adventure journal years ago after the movie "Up" came out on video. If you aren't familiar, the movie encourages adventures both big and small. In our journal, we write the adventurous things we've done together. You can keep this in your kitchen drawer, in your backpack or in the car's glove box. Just don't forget to keep it close at hand so you remember to make new adventures all the time.

- **Create an "I CAN" can.** We recently let the girls make "I Can" cans. I printed out "I can __" strips, and they fill in the blanks on what they can do. We brainstormed the list on our easel, but I was proud of the fact that one of my girls really took this project to heart and came up with her own ideas that weren't on our original list. This idea could easily be adjusted for an older age range. Film a video of what they can do. Design a book with photos of all the things they can do.

- **Celebrate.** I'm an avid light-a-candle mom. We light candles for the simplest things that we want to sparkle and let shine in our hearts. It's often for when we've done something brave or tried something new. We light candles for the baby steps we are all taking each week to push ourselves to be risk takers.

- **Talk it Out.** We talk a lot about what it means to be afraid and how it is really great to try new things. Notice when they take a risk. Point it out to them and see how their faces light up with just the notion that YOU noticed them being brave. It's a beautiful thing.

- **Release your own fears.** We absolutely push our fears onto our children. I have a fear of spiders. I try very hard not to show that fear too much. We have to really catch ourselves doubting our children's abilities because of our self-doubts. Yes, they might fall into the water if they get too close, but should we stop them from enjoying that amazing view? Yes, they might fall off their bike if they lose control while going too fast, but should we lock up their bike? Of course not. Risks are risks. They are all possible, and they are all worth doing.

- **Let them try.** The hardest of the hard. As your children are pulling away, let them go. It will only prepare all of you for phases to come. Trust that they know their way. Trust that they will do the right thing. Trust that if they do not, you can help guide them on better ways in the future.

> **Savoring Slow Invitation:** Let their play be your play today. Let their ideas be your ideas. Let their games be your games. Let their laughter inspire your laughter. Just follow their lead today. See how far they take you on a journey down Mindful Lane.

Unstructured quiet time

We all know those days when a baby won't nap aren't easy or fun.

The child will be cranky later on, and it throws off your entire day.

Except if you look at nap time as quiet unstructured time. Safety, of course, has to come first. But putting a child in their crib or bed with toys to play with is a great way to give them unstructured quiet time.

All of these tools give children the strength they need to be on their own as adults. They may still be young but they are taking baby steps to being independent. One of the things one of my girls wrote on her "I Can" paper was that she can go places by herself.

I was puzzled by this since she's never alone. So I asked her, "Where do you go by yourself?" She answered wisely, "I can go to

birthday parties by myself. I was scared but I went, and I did it."
She's right. She was dropped off for the first time last weekend.

I would not have thought of adding that to the list of things she could do, but she knew it was a risk that she took, that we both took. I may not ever be able to completely stop worrying, but I can certainly give my children the tools they need to find a balance of being cautious yet abundantly, amazingly and awesomely courageous.

Savoring Slow Habit No. 9 | Go Quiet

"Often we think that burnout is something that just happens to other women — to workaholics and perfectionists. But careaholics are also at risk — women who care deeply about their children, work, relationships, parents, siblings, friends, communities, issues." — Sarah Ban Breathnach

***

I was making breakfast the other day.

By breakfast, I mean un-toasted bagels with half peanut butter and half Nutella because that's what my daughters like most days of the week.

And it was one of those mornings you could literally hear the rain drops hitting the table outside.

Slow. Peaceful. Simple.

I have met a lot of mothers like myself who have a noise sensitivity. This sensitivity is a very real experience for me, and I've only noticed it since I became a mother and learned to value quiet so very much.

And so in our home, it's often pretty quiet — at least compared to many homes.

The thing is, though, that my children appreciate that quiet, too. Even the lone extrovert of our bunch. We all need it. And crave it.

Why?

Because it makes sense to us that when the rest of the world is crazy, loud and busy, we're able to control our senses a bit more by just tuning everything out and being alone together either in the same room or in the same house and just enjoying no noise.

Going quiet simply allows the world to finally rest. It allows us to finally rest.

Believe it or not, we have to work our habit-building muscles and remember to go quiet each day or else we will just forget.

That feeling of never having time to really think and soak in the silence contributes greatly to that feeling of tired, but awake — exhausted, but not ready to settle down to sleep, but also not energized to do much else.

There are quite a few ways to put this back into your days if you aren't doing it now — yes, even if you have a house full of kids. In fact, it can start with the kids right on your lap.

Build in quiet togetherness moments

Every day, when I expect my daughters to arrive home from school, I wait for them outside and meditate.

By meditate, I mean bringing myself back to center, breathing, and focusing my eyes on the grass, the trees, the sky, the clouds — anything that is right here, right now. This transition is a much-needed moment after spending so much of my day thinking about the future and sitting at the computer, writing and creating. I live in my head too much as it is, so this meditation is one that I use often to bring me back to my life.

Because being right here, right now is important to me when my children are around. And once they are home, more often than not, our afternoons and weekends are filled with creative learning and play. I zip in and out of their worlds, and they do the same in mine. It's an ebb and flow that isn't always perfect, but always works in some strange, mysterious way.

But tonight we were off.

The signs of a Family Funk were obvious.

Irritability. Restlessness. Frustration. Bickering. Asking for a lot of TV. Bad attitudes. Stubbornness. Tears. Lots and lots of tears.

Years ago, I would have let this kind of night tear me apart. Such high expectations. Such hopes for a peaceful night — as if they should all always be so perfect.

No longer do I let these fleeting moments take over my life.

And while they always do seem like the end of the world at the time, they are always fleeting. Thankfully.

Instead, I have learned to listen closely. I ask myself a series of questions. I start to problem solve. I retreat to my special quiet space. And I breathe through the mystery and try to unravel the puzzle.

Some days feel longer than others, and it's often on those really long days when I reach into my parenting toolbox and stretch myself and challenge myself on how creative I can really be as a mother — to help them move through this kind of a phase. For the longest time, I would begin creating family fun activities for the entire night, thinking it would be the best remedy out of a place of struggle as a family. Often, my own creativity and playfulness is all it takes to change the mood and tone of a moment like this.

But not this night. This night called for serious mama intervention.

We began with a much-earlier-than-normal dinner and then a straight shot to the couch, under the coziest blanket we own and with just our family room twinkle lights shining on us in the dark, we sat there in the stillness, being in quiet togetherness.

There wasn't a noise in the house other than the giggling under the blanket. Not even music. Just a dog barking in the distance.

"We should play some music," one of my girls said.

"I am enjoying the quiet," I said, slouched down between their warm bodies.

"Me, too," they both agreed.

When that moment passed, as they always do because of not enough blanket on one person, I moved upstairs.

They followed, as I knew they would, as I knew they needed to do. They are like little ducklings that way.

And we all piled onto my bed in our pajamas and fuzzy socks and read and wrote independently and hardly said a word to each other until it was time for bed. We sat close together. I could feel their breath on my arms. I read. One of them wrote a note for daddy, who was working late. And the other moved from a series of things that made her happy.

Sometimes quiet togetherness is really what we all need more than anything else.

And this quiet togetherness is almost always the most awake I ever feel as a mother.

The ability to stay connected and do our own thing while being there for each other. It's a precious moment that is surely to snap any of us out of our soul fever ... at least after a long night's sleep.

Savoring Slow Invitation: Go out of your way to set up a "quiet togetherness" moment today. Grab the things you know will keep everyone happy and quiet at the same time, and put them all in your favorite cozy gathering spot. Sit there and start doing your quiet thing. Invite the kids to join you when they enter the room.

Tuning out the noise of the world

About five years ago, I had this really big a-ha! moment.

You know, the life-changing kind.

I was came across this quote from Sarah Ban Breathnach.

"Often we think that burnout is something that just happens to other women — to workaholics and perfectionists. But careaholics are also at risk — women who care deeply about their children, work, relationships, parents, siblings, friends, communities, issues."

A careaholic?

Someone who cares too much for, among many things – community and issues?

I'd never heard of the term before. But the second I read it, it resonated with me wholeheartedly. That's me! That defines everything about me.

Well, the old me.

I have done a complete 360-degree turn.

That a-ha! moment really opened my eyes to the amount of time and energy I was putting into everything — and everyone and every cause and every issue — and not myself. Not my family. Not my own well being.

Many of those issues we all find ourselves submerged in land us flat in the Land of Bitter and Sour. A place of constant negativity.

Once I began cutting out the noise, my life opened up wide for more things I wanted to do. I finally finished my novel. I started a blog. I started teaching e-courses. I made more time for my kids and the things that made us happy.

Life changed instantly.

This information we receive constantly and repeatedly from the vast world of the Internet — the support, the ideas, the inspiration, the happy feelings, the friendships — is wonderful, and there is absolutely a place for it all in our lives. But, it's coming at us full-speed all day long.

It's the world we live in now. It's not going to change anytime soon. I love it. You love it. I am a better woman/mother/creative person for it all.

But we learn how to balance all of that information and how it's flying at us and understand both how to filter it and use it appropriately.

Go on a real information diet

The busier you are, the more tapped in to the world you are because you are out there, with people, all the time. And people talk.

They share information like that great summer camp your child should sign up for and how their child is the youngest child to win the championship of every sport around.

The real diet that should take place in your life is the information diet.

The diet that limits the amount of information you are bringing into your world.

This is how we build our quiet habit.

We don't just build our quiet habit sitting on a cushion. We have to prevent the noise from even entering our minds.

When we think about where the noise is coming from, though, we have to be selective. It can come from many sources — some of which we cannot control as easily.

When I first cut out TV, I thought it was great for my productivity to not be sitting in front of a table staring at a black box for an hour.

But the truth was that the TV watching was only a portion of the time I gained. The rest came directly from the fact that I wasn't getting all worked up over the news anymore. I didn't know about the latest homicide in the area. I was not seeing commercials for movies I just had to see in a theater.

The noise was just shushed.

The temptations were gone.

The world became quieter.

I still read the newspaper, where I am able to control how much I learn and when I move on, unlike on TV.

But even then, it's pretty minimal because I like my world quiet and free of noise from outside sources that will deplete my motherhood and creative energy.

Motherhood is hard work as it is. And being a creative writer and business owner, I need every ounce of energy I have left after the children are asleep or at school.

I simply do not have time for the noise.

I suspect you probably don't either.

> Savoring Slow Invitation: Go on a media or cause elimination diet. You might not want to do both, but you might easily find that one connects to the other. Choose a cause — or a media outlet — that consumes your mind more than you'd like. Social media and blogs could easily be on that list if that's where you are getting your information. Choose to take baby steps away from that outlet in an attempt to take more control of the noise that enters your head. If you need that information, is there another way or another time to get it rather than all day, every day?

The Research Department at home

We get an idea. We go to the computer. We look up the idea. We get our answer.

Then we spend the next half hour researching it further. To compare it even deeper. Then we start reading about it. And finding other examples and the problems and the complaints and that all leads to the Facebook page and the Pinterest accounts. Before we know it, we're almost able to write a dissertation on how to get our child potty trained.

Many of us are obsessed with information. We want the best prices and deals. We need the coupon. And we need free shipping so we search for codes for all of this before we move forward with our purchase so we can save $10.

But research costs something, too.

Your time.

It's one thing to look something up quickly and another to look something up and get sidetracked for hours with so much information that you are now rendered clueless and unable to make a decision.

This is all more noise in your head. More doubts. More fears. More worries. More dreads. More stress.

And to really think about it, the information you needed was found within the first five or ten minutes of looking up your topic. It's the rest — the distractions — that took your time.

Mindful computer use is not just about social media, though we definitely use that more than most platforms. But pure research is another time stealer of your day. If you want more time back, stop looking up so many things.

This goes for minor medical conditions, too.

Obviously, if you have a major health diagnosis and your life depends on knowing what's out there to live better, that's different. But how many of us spend too much time looking up our symptoms of minor things?

This is all noise, too. Noise in your head that makes you worry and dread what is yet to come.

- The News.

- Blogs.

- Social Media.

- Photo sharing.

- Dr. Google.

- The next best recipe.

- DIY cold remedies.

I am not proposing a full-blown Internet fast — you know, when you just completely give up on all devices for a week or a month. And then sit and twiddle your thumbs. And when you return — the next week or the next month — you will feel so refreshed that you're going to jump right back in 100 percent knowing full well that you will burnout on it all again.

I'm proposing that you can learn to find the balance between offline and online in your everyday life so that it doesn't fully consumes your mind and give you information burnout.

The secret to balancing all of this information, though, is in the release — the quieting of your own mind from the information overload.

For example, if you spend a lot of time finding recipes online to make for your family, take a weekend to make those recipes. Keep the good ones, toss the bad ones. And promise yourself you won't search for any new ones until you've tried the ones you have already bookmarked or printed.

If you take in something with your mind, if you feel a lot of feelings (and we all do!), those feelings and that information needs to be released or expressed or reflected upon.

You need to do something with all of that information in your head. Choosing to consciously go quiet rather than taking in more and more information is the key to more Savoring Slow moments.

> Savoring Slow Invitation: Set a timer. Research your biggest need right now. See how long it takes to get your answer. And then practice stopping yourself when you have what you need rather than researching it to death.

Solitude

Teaching children to understand their own noise and busyness boundaries is such a powerful tool to offer.

A child who can sense when they are becoming too overstimulated is a child who can regulate their own emotions better in the long run.

Of course teaching this skill — or awareness — is not something that can be done in one day but rather over a long period of time. Maybe even their entire childhood.

Even extroverted children who need constant companionship become overstimulated and need down time. The kind of downtime they need may vary, but a dose of solitude is always good for the soul.

At our house, we have put to use a number of tools over the years to help our twin daughters cope with needing to be away from each other — or away from the entire family.

All of these ideas can be adapted to meet your own child's needs.

Our days are so full. Filled with energy and lists with the most obscure things to fit in, like clean the toilet and weed the flower bed.

It can be easy to put off "just be" on your own to-do list, but that's exactly what you need if you want to savor a much slower way of life.

Yes, the dishes need to be done, the work is piling up and the children need your attention. But your ability to maintain it all with positive energy begins with you and taking time to go quiet.

To go quiet, focus on these 5 simple ways to quiet your mind:

1. **Write it out.** Take everything you've thought about, worried about, gotten angry about, felt disappointed about or even really excited about and write it all down in the form of crazy, informal, ungrammatically correct sentences. Dump it all, no matter what time of day you are in. This exercise works while drinking coffee as much as it works while laying in bed waiting for sleep to come. I've also done my fair share at 4 a.m. when I couldn't sleep. If sentences won't form, write lists. Lots and lots of lists.

2. **Walk it out.** Walk until the thoughts start to slow down. Until the pictures — the choices, the decisions — all become clearer. Walk until things just start to make sense to you.

3. **Breathe it out.** Find yourself a meditation or relaxation video or CD and lay down flat and rest. Be at ease. Chill out. Stop thinking. Let it all fall down through the earth. Let every muscle relax.

4. **Create it out.** Make something — you know, with your hands. Create something. You never have to show another human being. Or perhaps you want to. Just pick your favorite thing to make and get busy making it.

5. **Zen it out.** Meditation comes in many forms. Sitting and breathing can be done on a cushion, a bench, a chair …

anywhere you can do nothing other than breathe in and breathe out. I call this doing nothing and yet I still find it so hard to work into my day.

Savoring Slow Habit No. 10 | Savor

"The journey is the reward." ~ Chinese Proverb

***

Savor the way the chocolate hits your tongue and the way the sun lights up the trees.

Savor the way the coffee smell drifts through the kitchen and the way you light up when you see your child's bed head.

Savor the way your bare feet slide on the cool floors and the way the blankets feel as you wrap them around you.

Savor the way he looks at you and the way the two of you dance around each other in perfect harmony.

Savor the day's work not as chores but as nesting and the way it all makes you feel when it's done.

Savor the taste of sweet carrots or juicy apples or crisp lettuce and the way it makes your body feel to eat it.

Savor the look of need in her eyes and the fact that you are still oh-so-needed.

Savor the bright moon and the magical stars and the mysteriousness of the darkness from your window before you sleep.

Savor it all.

Every bit of it.

Savoring the moment as if it's the last one is my favorite way to create a slower pace of time in my life. I love to wake early and walk outside and smell the grass and watch for birds while drinking my coffee with two hands.

This is the only way I know how to cherish every single season — both the real seasons outside and my own.

What I know to be true is that the more we slow down and get lost in the moment — from toasting the bagel and spreading the peanut butter to fluffing the pillows and straightening the blankets — the more we fall back in love with our life.

In my own home, I have seasons where I'm skimming the surface, climbing so close to the top gasping for air because I have so much on my mind.

And then the season changes, and I'm wakened again as if to see for the very first time.

What would we do without the change of seasons? I can't imagine being in a place where this didn't happen. And even in those places, where the snow doesn't fall, there are seasons of another kind.

Savoring the quirks of a family

There are many phases that come and go in a family life, just as there are many seasons that run through motherhood and childhood, too.

The key is to simplify, embrace the chaos and understand these seasons and how they affect your daily flow and rhythm — and how busy we feel.

I personally fall into a new season every several weeks, and then

I wonder what happened to that rhythm I was so happily trotting along in just the week before.

In a flash, everything changes.

My energy. My mood. My motivation. My social radar. My mothering skills. My wife skills. My cleaning ambitions.

Poof. Gone.

I speak a lot about the seasons of motherhood because I've paid enough attention in my own life to be able to recognize a dry season. The season that leaves me less than stellar, less than motivated, less than creative, less than productive.

And I've learned to ride the dry season as long as I need to.

That often means an earlier bedtime. Fewer blog posts. More bouts of doing not much of anything.

Over the years, I've learned to understand my own seasons and how they ebb and flow. Some seasons fly in with a vengeance and leave with a gust. Others tip-toe in softly and knock me down without warning as if an iron pot was crashed over my head.

But here's the thing: I couldn't be without all these seasons of myself. Not the real me.

I couldn't be the mother I've become. So I embrace all of them with the fiercest of grips because I know from experience they won't last long. I relish in the way they wake me up and change me. I savor their challenges and soft pushes for me to become just a little bit better.

And then they pass.

When they pass I see the new me and stand ready for the next season to weather me some more.

Savoring the seasons our family goes through — the way we all nestle in by the fire in the winter and read books, or the way we all roam wild and free in the summer doing our own thing — shows us new glimpses at what it means to live a slow, meaningful life.

We no longer rush by and hurry through, we stop and we listen, we stop and we stare, we stop and we focus.

And there is so much for a family to cherish. The way we walk around each other in the kitchen or the bathroom. The way we interrupt each other when we're excited. The way we grouch at each other when we're tired.

These everyday things can often feel frustrating when dealing with them day after day, but they are your family's quirks, they are what make you uniquely you.

These quirks and personality traits and idiosyncrasies make us real and authentic, and that is all something to savor as our children grow up because they will remember how you walked in the room and greeted them or how you worked all day to try and hang a swing.

These frustrations aren't easy to cope with, but they are worth remembering, worth savoring.

In the corner of my office, there are piles of everyone's clutter. Things they no longer want. And they get dumped in my space because it's the leftover room of the house. The in-between.

This gathering and piling is a season straight out of the hunter's and gatherer's era, I'm sure.

And then we'll flow into a new season — the one where we will clear space, clear mind, in order to feel renewed and reinvigorated for our home space again.

There are more seasons than just that one for a family. We have an active season, where we take on more than we should. And then we have the paring-down season, where we let go of many things to make more time to be at home.

This is a part of our flow as a family. Perhaps, some day, the habits will change and we'll create new seasons.

But the point is that these are, indeed, habits we've created and now live with as a part of our family fabric. I embrace them not as a burden or as an obstacle to a better life.

I savor them and embrace them as my life. As our authentic place in this world.

> **Savoring Slow Invitation:** This week, see if you can detect your own seasons or your family's seasons. Write them down as you notice them and keep them in a safe place for your own information to use this same time next year or next month. You don't need to do anything but observe and take note of what you are all going through right now.

Savoring your own moods and seasons

One of my more favorite seasons is actually my least productive season.

It's the slow season. The exhausted season. This is the season when I sit back and let the world unfold around me.

It's the early-to-bed, late-to-rise season. The dishes-are-still-in-the-sink and the lunches-are-not-made season. The pay-for-it-in-the-morning season. These ebb and flow more frequently than I'd like and often follow a nice "I got this" season.

I'm pretty sure there is a direct correlation there. I have learned to love this season most of all because it means I have needs that are not addressed and to honor those needs is the biggest way I can take care of myself. I have also learned that the best way to move through this season is to sleep right on through it.

Consider, for a minute, your own seasons. Those phases you find yourself in time and time again and you wonder if you're crazy or weird or lazy.

Zero in on that season that might be your slow season. You probably spend a lot of time beating yourself up on what you're not doing in that season. You're probably thinking you have to get it together, you have to be more productive.

But what your body is telling you is that you need to slow down. To rest. To soak in the tub or lay in your bed a while longer.

Listen to your personal seasons and what they tell you. Your inner wisdom is talking to you.

And if you let the whispers wash over you, you might find a harmony of slow that is already inside of you, waiting to be let loose, waiting to be free of all the adult burdens you are carrying around.

Fall in love with the seasons outside

I can — and have — written something beautiful about every single season.

This wasn't the case when I was younger, but I'm on a mission to help my children see the good and the bad of life. The light and the dark. The happy and the sad.

Seasons weather us. They weather our family lives. They weather our homes.

We are changed after every single season in one way or another.

And there is so much to savor about each season. So much to fall in love with. So much to relish and appreciate.

Summer is full of catching fireflies, staying up late and walking barefoot.

Fall is full of beautiful leaves, crisp, cool air for deep breaths and long hikes through the woods.

Winter is full of going inward, reflecting and dreaming. Fires in the fireplace. S'mores over the stove. And the holidays that keep us feeling bright and cheery.

Spring is full of renewal and rebirth. Beautiful colors and blue skies. And full of feelings of hope that we can move about the earth again.

There is truly something to be savored about every single season.

Here's the thing: It's not the weather. It's your mindset about the weather.

I know because I am one of those anti-snow people. I have never liked the stuff. And it dates back to being a child with a February birthday and many of my birthday parties being cancelled as a foot or more of snow piled on the ground.

But I've come to appreciate winter and all weather patterns. I may not like them, but I can tolerate them so much more than I used to. Same goes for the heat of the summer. The rain of the spring. And the ... well, fall is usually just perfect, isn't it?

Appreciate the season you're in. Yes, the actual season but also the mothering season you're in, as well. This is the place you are right now as you deal with the phases your children are in. They don't always mesh. They just are. Let them be. There are good things and bad things about every single season. Notice the beauty, honor what you love and focus on that. For instance, winter is such a great time for family connection and internal reflection. Go there. Forget about what you can't do.

Stop controlling everything. The weather is the best gift for telling us who's boss. We're not in charge of the Universe, no matter how hard we try to be. But we are in charge of how we use our time, what we let our mind focus on and what we choose to be happy about. Releasing the hold that simple things like weather patterns have over us is a step in the journey of letting go to all the little things that shape us and hold our minds captive.

Surrender. Surrender to the fact that this is your normal – this totally abnormal, can't-keep-up-with-what's-happening kind of schedule. It's always something with kids. Always. If it's not snow storms or heat waves, it's illnesses, broken limbs, job losses, school changes and other bits of chaos. But those missed days at work will be made up with more family memories. Missed school will be made up in better weather. And life will go on as it always does.

Bring out your best. This is your time to shine. Prove to yourself that you are Super Mom just as you are and you're not going to let this weather bring you down. It's just weather. It's not forever. Put that on a bumper sticker!

Savoring Slow Invitation: Create a Seasons' binder. One of my favorite ways to capture the seasons and really savor them slowly is to create a Seasons' binder — a binder where you will keep all of the beautiful things you love about each season. Recipes. Activities. Traditions. Lists. Photos. Journal pages.

Savoring Slow Habit No. 11 | Abundance

"True forgiveness is when you can say, "Thank you for that experience." — Oprah Winfrey

***

I found abundance, once, in a field of rhododendrons.

My daughters and I were hiking during their summer break. I had just quit my full-time job in politics to stay home and expand my family wellness coaching practice.

And the feeling of abundance washed over me as we saw those flowers in the middle of the field.

I was right where I needed to be.

We had reduced our earned income by a significant amount at the time to make things work. But all I wanted was to raise my children and show them the world.

Abundance doesn't mean cash or thick wallets.

Abundance means love of life, and it is often discovered in our slowest, most simple moments

When you stop chasing after what you don't have and start thinking like someone who has everything they need, you start realizing you don't have that much to race toward — at least not at a record-breaking pace.

When you know you already have everything you need, your life instantly feels full of abundance.

Being grateful is so much more than listing a few things. It's truly a habit you must form and believe in to feel the true benefits.

Nearly four years ago, I set an intention to begin a practice of gratitude.

It read like this:

> May I feel real gratitude flowing through my body. May I accept what has been handed to me and love every moment through and through.

Here's what I've learned from this gratitude practice:

- Time slows down when I stop to appreciate it more.
- When you experience a loss, gratitude helps you move through it more quickly.
- Strangers do amazing things for us.
- Life becomes so much clearer and more joyful.

These little moments of grace offer a sense of peace in a hard, crazy life. And now, I rarely stop at five things each night. I often write close to 10. Maybe I'm just more aware.

Maybe these gifts of gratitude were always here. Maybe they are new. Each one, though, is like a tiny snowflake — unique, different and precious.

Abundance leads to a slower pace

Lately, when I'm feeling overwhelmed, I have a pact with myself: Go walk in the grass and stand under a tree.

Sometimes, that's all it takes to wake me up and snap me out of it.

Clarity arrives sooner or later.

It always, always does.

Mothers put too much pressure on themselves. On their lives. On the people around them.

I know I cannot be alone in this.

So we lean in on the mistakes, the imperfections, the less thans, and we get into that negative bubble.

The only way to snap out of it is to get out of your head.

So go walk in the grass and say thanks for this life.

Stand under a tree. Write poetry. Read. Watch ants at work. Listen for the birds busy nesting. And realize that you are not alone in trying to make things happen.

We're always trying to make things happen.

But real life ... it's out in the grass, under the clouds ... that's where poetry can be found.

Sometimes, I just sit and watch nothing and take in everything I already have in my life, and I am overwhelmed with a feeling of abundance.

This is when I am most at peace, in this sitting and taking it all in.

The world around me could be falling apart, but if I can tune it all out and see the good, I know I am on the right track in my day.

Some days, admittedly, this is harder to do.

I attribute my ability to sit and take it all in — and feel immense abundance — to my own gratitude practice.

To do one more thing might seem contradictory to savoring

slow, but learning to find the abundance in your life is actually the epitome of savoring slow.

And yet what is most beautiful about a deep, profound gratitude practice is that it can be done anywhere, literally.

A practice of gratitude and abundance leads your heart to its natural, content state.

You will always wish for things to be different, but you will absolutely do less of that thinking.

A gratitude practice can be as simple and basic — or as deep and lovely — as you wish it to be in your life.

It can become your spiritual practice.

It can be your writing practice.

It can be your mothering center.

It can be a journal or a scrapbook or just a calendar of notes.

The point is not the what.

The point is the feeling. The point is the residue of a beautiful life left on your skin after a long walk in the warm sun. The point is the red stains of strawberries on her lips and finger tips after a day of picking. The point is the long hug at the end of the tantrum.

The point is never the list and always the feeling of being awake and noticing.

The rest of this chapter will invite you to practice finding abundance in many places in your day — your regular, busy day.

Start in bed

The first place to start practicing abundance is right there, in your bed when you wake up in the morning and before you start your day.

We can help ourselves find more peace in our days when we

take just a moment to close our eyes and rest in stillness for all that is about to unfold in our day and all that is sure to go right.

This is not a moment for dread of what is going to unravel or go wrong. Nor is this a moment to hurry up and rush through what needs to be done all day.

Slowing down how we see our day unfolding can be a powerful way to live a slower life. It can be the difference between seeing a blur of noise and movement and seeing beauty blossoming right before your eyes.

Start in the shower

This is not a writing prompt, though you could find some way to turn it into that as well. This is about using your time in the shower — a task we all do routinely — to let abundance wash over you. Much like the meditation in the shower, you simply use this time to think about what is happening in your life that you are grateful for — before you even begin your day.

This undivided attention is a great time to start listening to the abundance in your life starting from the minute you wake up to the minute you go to bed.

- Warm, clean water.

- Fresh towels.

- A door to shut and lock out the world.

- A comfortable bed and blankets.

- Modern luxuries.

With every item you list, consume your mind with how great it feels to have what you need and not need anything more.

It's that simple.

We have what we need. We don't need anything more.

Start with your coffee

The darkness was thick in our kitchen. I shuffled my favorite grey fleece socks over the cold tiled floor.

And went straight to the coffee pot, my best friend each and every morning.

Each sound resonated in my ears.

With the warm cup in my hands, I stared out at the moon. The bright stars. The clear blue sky. Winter's grip had been too much to bear. And yet there was so much stillness. I turned on soft music. I lit a candle. I read a meditation. And then I wrote one for myself.

As each sip of warm fluid went down my throat, I was fully aware, fully awake, fully present.

This was one morning that felt intentional and beautiful. It was the perfect start to an imperfect day.

It was the one moment I had complete control over for my own happiness.

Soon, my daughter shuffled into the room, wrapped in her own white fleece blanket, hair on end from static and a smile like no other.

Let the day begin.

Start with the hard

I don't think anyone goes into raising a child thinking it will be easy.

They just think their version of a child will be easier — and not like the others, not like those crying babies in the grocery store. And then they have a child. And wake up.

From there, it's a constant battle between which bottle to choose to what organic foods to serve to how many hours can we let them nap before it ruins tonight's sleep.

In other words, it still becomes a lot about us and our needs.

And while we all shout to new parents to enjoy every second, we know the truth is that many will not because it is hard.

And no one likes hard things.

Our body's natural coping mechanism with anything that is hard is to move through it as quickly and painlessly as possible. Close your eyes, it will pass soon.

Raising children — particularly two or more — is hard work.

It's requires constant time management, negotiations and being on all the time — for nearly two decades.

So when I say we must savor the hard, do the hard, I mean it.

The trick is to feel the emotions, work your way through them and realize that this is your life. This is raising a child.

It's not going to suddenly get easier.

The only thing that will change is that the years seem to get shorter.

They get taller.

Their personalities evolve, and you start wondering how you'll cope without them in your life because ... they are your life.

So when I say savor the hard.

Do the hard.

Start with your children

Our children are always just doing their jobs — being children.

That means they are both curious and full of energy, but also selfishly looking out for their best interests.

It can be hard to swallow to see a child making choices from an ego-point of view, but it's not meant to be personal.

There are so many fun ways to get children to open up to the idea of being grateful and noticing the abundance in their own lives.

It begins, of course, with how we, the parents, demonstrate how we see the gifts we've been given, first of all.

If I demonstrate immense gratitude for the fact that my husband has a good job, even though he's home late most nights, they will understand the value that job has in our lives and in our family.

It's just a shift in our mindset, and children can learn it easily.

To get you started, here are a few fun ideas to draw children into the world of abundance.

- **Be a Gratitude Role Model.** When you spend every night writing all your blessings into a journal, you're bound to pass along the gratitude basket to your children. Saying these blessings out loud to them only reinforces this type of modeling. "I'm so happy you are in my life." "I'm so honored to have good friends." "Your Dad is the best Dad in the world." "I am so grateful to get to spend my day with you."

- **Simplicity matters.** Keep things simple, and children are bound to start noticing the little things in life. We don't have a lot of fancy things. We only just got our first big-screen TV last year, and that was a really big deal. When we bought our newish minivan, it was another really big deal. We aren't splashy. We aren't contrived. We just live and try to make a difference in our community every day. The rest is a bonus. We are passing this along to our children delicately while also helping them achieve their own dreams.

- **Talk about the world.** Talk about how the rain is important to the flowers. Talk about how we get our food. Talk about the importance of Sunday morning pancakes. Talk about what matters to your children. Help them see the world from a different perspective that reminds them to be grateful.

- **Teach actions.** Saying thank you is fine. It is. But in these busy, crazy times of social networking and little connection to real people, it's important to teach children to show up and give thanks. Have them write out their thank yous daily in a journal. Call instead of emailing. Give cookies to the school janitor.

- **Give thanks.** For all children, writing or drawing a picture of the things they are thankful for is a great way to get them thinking about being thankful. For the ones not quite ready for that kind of daily devotion, a simple bedtime ritual works wonders. Ask your child what she is grateful for today. Share your own idea or two with her as well.

- **Make cards.** Every now and then, I buy blank cards and let the girls go crazy with decorating them any way they want. We send those cards to the people in our life who need a lift. Thank you cards are a lost art that some of us really wish people would spend more time on. Make a card. Give thanks daily. Spread joy weekly.

Savoring Slow Invitation: Create a gratitude bulletin board in your home. Encourage everyone to leave notes of thanks for things, experiences, ideas and successes – – as well as for the basics we all take for granted. Start the board yourself and see how the family takes to it over time.

Savoring Slow Habit No. 12 | Make Space

"Time is a created thing. To say 'I don't have time,' is like saying, 'I don't want to." — Lao Tzu

***

The other day, instead of rushing my daughters' upstairs for pajamas and bed, they asked to go play in the rain. I said yes, reluctantly. And, once again, I learned the value of making space for living in the moment.

They were outside in the rain for a long time — at least a half hour. They had rain coats on and they ran and jumped in puddles, rushing and saving worms from drowning on the tiny sidewalk rivers. ??I think about this moment a lot, especially when I realize I want more of these moments, not less.

I want more living.

More time for spontaneous surprises that have never happened before.

More time to do what feels good and less time for what doesn't.

In her new book, "Overwhelmed: Work, Love and Play When No One Has the Time," Washington Post journalist Brigid

Schulte talks about that flow we all desire that includes long stretches of free time. She she calls it time serenity.

Serenity can happen in many ways, but I'll admit I am my own worst enemy at leaving space for serendipitous moments to occur in my life. And yet my favorite word is serendipity.

How do we balance everything that needs to be done with leaving more space — more serenity — for the good stuff?

This whole book has walked you through the how to savor the slow moments. But it hasn't shown you how to grasp more slow moments by the hand and lead them on a long, gentle walk.

By building a habit of creating space in our days — and our minds — for savoring the slow we are building a lifetime of creating amazing opportunities for ourselves and our children.

So, perhaps, I've saved the best for last. I've given you all the tools I know to enjoy today for what it is, and now I'm going to try and convince you to actually carve out the space in your day for these things that matter to you.

Physically making space for Savoring Slow

I love to create places and spaces that inspire creativity and stillness and peace in our home. You may have figured this out by my creative spaces Pinterest board. And in all of my e-courses, I've always gone on and on and on about creating a space of our own as mothers.

In our home, we have a chalkboard on the door from our kitchen to the garage. We have a peace corner. We have an art cabinet. A writing box. A storytelling basket. A reading nook.

And I love to see my daughters create their own special spaces, too.

In fact, just today as I write this, the hallway leading to my room was decorated with a trail of stale jelly beans they found hidden in a nook of something and a baby doll seated next to a candle now graces my bathroom sink.

Creating nooks and crannies that offer a place to sit quietly, reflect and create as a family is one of my favorite tools for practicing living an awake life, especially at home. These special family spaces are cozy and peaceful and open to conversation and spending time together. The best spaces are the ones where there will be no distractions of a television or a computer.

It's when we sit in this kind of stillness together and laugh in joy when we feel what a slower life can do for our family's well being.

Savoring Slow Invitation: Create a family space that speaks of Savoring Slow. Create one inside and outside when the weather permits. Once it's created, use it for what it is intended. Make a point to sit in that space and be still as often as possible. This is a great space to pause, journal and reflect on the abundance in your life.

The value of a good list

Once again, I return to lists.

Lists keep me happy. I don't carry my list around on a clipboard, checking off everything and looking to add new things all the time. Not even close. A list, for me, is a memory jogger, and that's it. It's there to remind me and pull me back on track when I get the time.

When I go into the moment with my children, it can be easy to put off everything else and then forget what needs to be done. A list brings me back to center.

That's it.

If something on my list doesn't get done, it gets moved to the next day's list, and no tears are shed.

The point is not to make a list of everything in all of creation that needs to get done and do it.

The point is to create a list that reminds you of what's important for today, for this day and this day only.

And so we need three essential lists to use in our lives in order to learn how to create the right kind of space in our days for savoring slow. No, you do not need to use these lists every day. Use them when you know you need them.

The Real Life List

I keep my real life list in a planner.

And next to my real life list are my other lists — along with what's for dinner tonight.

My real life list includes things like dentist appointment and pick up potato salad for the teacher luncheon at my daughters' school. My real life list includes work deadlines and life deadlines — deadlines that need to be met or else.

My real life list isn't always fun. It isn't fancy. It isn't much to brag about — it's just the stuff of life, the ordinary gifts I've been given, like checking the garden and sending reminders to others for things they need to do. I try to keep my real life list short each day with three or four things being the most that ever goes on it. More than that, and I'll feel overwhelmed.

This list is your list. The one everyone keeps. But it's not the most important list.

That's next.

> Savoring Slow Invitation: There are going to be many things on your real life list that you do not like. While you may get lucky and find ways out of them, accept that most of those things are there to stay, and you need to refer back to the habits of savoring and going slowly and reframing.

The Thinking Mama's To-Do List

The Thinking Mama's To-Do List is the real list that will shape the best parts of your life. The one that tells you what you want to be doing instead of everything on that real life list.

This is the list you will want to refer to often in your day or your afternoon after work. This is the list to pay attention to because it is the list that matters.

On my own Thinking Mother's List right now, I have the following:

- Play together

- Learn together

- Be active

- Be silly

- Read together

- Tell stories from the past

- Create something

- Show your love

- Be grateful

The reason I began creating this kind of list — and it's the kind of list I made once and use often — is because I get caught up in the day-to-day stuff and, like anyone, forget about the stuff that matters.

There are more things we can add to this list but these are the actions I want to take each day. And the more I thought about that, the more I wanted to do another list that put more things on my list of to-dos. Not in a pressure-me kind of way but in a oh, yeah, that's right, here's the big picture right now, here's what matters.

- Say I love you.

- Write little notes.

- Tell jokes.

- Remember to laugh.

- Linger at bedtime

- Take one-on-one time, even if just five minutes.

- Journal back-and-forth.

- Write down one good thing they did.

- Write down one good thing I did.

And suddenly, the more I thought about these positive things I wanted to do with my family, the more I recognized that all the other things on my real life list seemed rather silly and mundane.

And a brilliant thing happened.

I started to do more of these fun, amazing things — the things that make motherhood fun and worth every moment.

It's amazing what power a list — a really good list — can hold on a single piece of paper.

Savoring Slow Invitation: Write down your own Thinking Mama's To-Do List. Write down all the things you want to do with or for your family this week or this month and keep the list next to your real list. Check it often and fit in all of the things through the week and through the month. Do not even try to do them all in one day. Think one per day or two, at most. Spread out the love.

The Busy Mama's To-Do List

This is that list that is always, always shoved to the back of the mini-van and put under the soccer cleats. It's that list of things you need to do for yourself, to feel happier and more rested and more joyful.

When we have newborns in the house, people urge us to sleep when they sleep. But what about as they get older, when they stop sleeping during the day? What about the rest of the time?

We're still exhausted. Overworked. And, under-appreciated.

Can we get five minutes of peace?

I've been thinking about self-care a lot lately. For myself. My good friends I'm hearing from who are struggling. For my work staff who are just now learning the joys and sorrows of working motherhood.

Since we're on a mission here of creating happy families, we must begin with ourselves. And that means dads, too.

So, in an effort to remind myself and all of you about taking care of ourselves, here are some of the things we need to do daily — or, at least weekly — to care for ourselves.

My own list is pretty simple. I don't need much to recharge.

Take time for ourselves.

For some, it might be a long walk. For others, it might be zoning out in front of a good book. For me, it's doing absolutely nothing. No noise is preferred. This is the only way I know that I will turn my overactive brain off for a while. Embrace silence. Let go.

- **Sleep.** Go to bed early, especially when you start to feel run down.

- **Eat well.** It's really easy to grab lunch out or skip meals, but we all know that is not the healthiest way to take care of our bodies. It's best to take time before you go to bed to pack or make yourself a healthful lunch.

- **Wake up happy.** The best way to wake up happy is to do one thing that fills you with energy and joy each and every morning. That usually means don't run to the computer and check email. Light a candle and meditate. Go for a run. Or do yoga.

- **Stay organized.** This is really key for me. I'm still not nearly as organized as I would like to be, but I've come a long, long way.

Every paper has a place. I have a good system for understanding what needs to be done today and what can wait until tomorrow, or even next week. Things still fall through the cracks, but not nearly as often.

The "I Will Not Do" List

Life's been busy. The sun is shining like a golden halo around the earth. Spring has sprung and I can only think of one thing: being out there under the big, big sky.

So I'm creating more time to embrace this Savoring Slow movement by creating a list of things I will not do.

Sometimes the best way to slow down is simply defining what we're not going to do.

What I Won't Do This Week:

- I won't oversleep and miss my quiet time when I sit with coffee, a journal and a pen near the cool breeze blowing through the window.

- I won't rush my girls unless it's an actual emergency. I won't lose my cool with anyone or let anyone ruin my day.

- I won't think angry thoughts about people.

- I won't worry about the cleaning when I could be lying in the grass watching the birds fly through the sky or digging in the garden.

- I won't criticize my husband no matter how late he gets home or how many times he falls asleep in the chair.

- I won't devalue myself and my worth by comparing myself to others or worrying about what they think of me.

Savoring Slow Invitation: Start a running list of the things you will not do today. Make them big and bold because the things you are doing that do not feel good aren't worth your time and energy. Consider putting things on your list that you have always wanted to do but just no longer have the energy or desire to work toward anymore — like being a published author or learning to roller skate.

Writing Your Ta Da! List

One of the biggest fears of many moms I know is that they are failing as mothers.

And these are some of the most creative, well-intentioned mothers out there.

And they think they are failing!

Raising children is no easy feat, and it's easy to think we're making mistake after mistake.

And we might be, at times.

That's why I created my absolute favorite productivity tool. The Ta-Da List! As in, Tada! — look what I did today. Let's set the record straight with ourselves. We do way more than we think in a day. We do way more good in a day than we're willing to admit sometimes, too.

In fact, the evidence in a ta-da list is really quite remarkable some days. How does this tie into our confidence as mothers?

Once you start writing all that you did and all that you accomplished, you start to feel better about the job you did all day. You start to see why you didn't have much time to do the things you wanted to do. You start to see the patterns on when you yell. You start to see how your mood flows into the rest of the family's moods. You start to see how you tried your best. You start to see how your work paid off.

All because you wrote a little list.

This is one of those lists that change you and your perception of how you are doing. You finally have proof of how you spent your time and how you did many things just perfectly right. That you were, indeed, a really good mom. And no one needs to see this list but you.

Savoring Slow Invitation: Close to bedtime, write down everything you accomplished that day instead of (or in addition to) everything you still need to do. Put lots of exclamation points on your list if you must. Do it again tomorrow and the next day to see the true impact on your confidence. No matter what … just be happy with your progress. Be happy you are so amazing. Because you are.

Conclusion: Make the Choice to Savor Slow

Nothing in life is worth rushing through because all of it is your life, even the dishes and the laundry.

Everything you have to do in a day, everything that has to be done to keep a happy, peaceful family it's all your life. That means you have to make a conscious decision to begin savoring the slow parts of your day, even the ones that last just mere minutes.

Families often reach burnout and overwhelm while trying to live a life that is beyond the one they already have happening right now. We're always waiting, hoping, dreaming and aspiring for something bigger, greater and better. And while we're so busy waiting for that future life to happen, we're missing the one that is happening right now all around us.

Savoring Slow requires new habits that will transform your busy life into something more tolerable and enjoyable.

By recognizing the parts you can slow down and do more intentionally, you are instantly creating more meaningful moments to capture and remember. For your family to have more time, you have to take control of your hours and start making them all count, even the really crazy moments.

So, simplify, embrace the chaos and find an abundance of time at home.

When you find yourself feeling tired and overwhelmed, and starting to worry and fear for the things you do not have any time for, just start back at the beginning and remind yourself of all the Savoring Slow habits.

You already have a perfect life. You already have what you need. Now start savoring it.

About the Author

Shawn Fink has been called the Yoda of Mamas. She is the founder of **The Abundant Mama Project**, an online community for busy mamas who want to be more peaceful, playful and present. She is also the author "**The Playful Family.**" Sign up to receive a weekly Wake Up and Pause email to remind you of what is most important and to learn about other ways to become an Abundant Mama — and grab your **FREE download of "The Abundant Mama 10 Habits of Highly Effective Mamas."** Get more inspiration on her website abundantmama.com.

Made in the USA
Middletown, DE
27 April 2017